Not Home

**The Companion Book to the Documentary about
Kids Living in Nursing Facilities**

Edited by

Narcel G. Reedus

Not Home Documentary, LLC
P.O. Box 9333
Charlotte, NC 28299

ISBN 978-0-9857268-0-5

Printed in USA by 48HrBooks (www.48HrBooks.com)
Cover Design: RL Design + Branding & PR (www.roslynlewis.com)

Thank You

I thank Elizabeth O'Berry for helping me understand that sometimes we do what needs to be done only because it is the right thing to do.

I thank my good friend Gillian Grable for
Inspiring me to take on this project.

I thank Katie Chandler her insight and direction.

I thank Joe Jowers for having a great eye.

I thank Judith Moen and John San Miguel
for their wisdom and knowledge.

I thank my wife Sheila Reedus for her love and support.

Table of Contents

Preface

This project started in the fall of 2009. Sheila and I were living in Texas and her job transferred her to Atlanta – my old stomping grounds for many years. I resigned my teaching position and began looking for employment in Atlanta. I contacted an old friend Gillian Grable who hired me years ago to direct and produce the short documentary *Waddie Welcome: A Man Who Cannot be Denied.* She told me about the Children's Freedom Initiative and their effort to get children out of nursing homes. I was a bit confused. "Why would there be children living in nursing homes?" I asked. Her first point of correction to me was that they are really not "homes" but more like facilities. I listened and thought that someone should make some kind of video or documentary on this subject. I didn't initially make the connection that that someone should be me. I was looking for work not a video project. Before graduate film school at Temple University I worked at the Georgia Advocacy Office as a Mental Health Advocate. I told Gillian I was open to going back into advocacy if a video position was not available.

I found myself in Atlanta still looking for employment. Gillian told me about the upcoming ADAPT rally in Atlanta. I believe this was the moment it occurred to me to embark upon this project. I knew there would be people from all over the country in Atlanta who could possibly speak about the issue of children in nursing facilities. I did not want to miss this opportunity.

I contacted Amber Smock at ADAPT and told her about the project and she put me in contact with a couple of people that were placed in institutions as a child. I had a couple of interviews scheduled. Great. I was on my way except I didn't have any funding or very much equipment. I had a mini DV camera and a tripod but I knew I would need lights and a microphone to conduct decent interviews. I contacted my old friend Joe Jowers – a fantastic D.P. (Director of Photography). He agreed to give me a hand. I somehow scrapped together enough cash to buy some used soft lights and a lavaliere microphone from a Craigslist ad. I actually hid this equipment in a closet fearful my wife wouldn't quite understand. Amber Smock let us use her hotel room to conduct the interviews and Joe and I shot footage of the ADAPT rally. It was amazing to see hundreds of folks marching from the CNN Center to the Martin Luther King, Jr. Center.

I edited that footage into a short promo video, got a website and started seeking funding. Josetta Shropshire, an old friend from Gary, Indiana, told me that the Georgia Council on Developmental Disabilities had some funding available for video projects. I sent Dottie Adams an email giving a brief explanation of the project – a documentary about kids living in nursing facilities. A day or two later I received an email from Dottie stating that the GCDD could give me a grant for $4,999. I was ecstatic.

Fast forward two years, 80 interviews, 200 hours of footage and seven states later: I took a full time position in North Carolina in part to self finance *Not Home: A documentary about kids living in nursing facilities.* I eventually received additional funding from the Georgia Advocacy Office, the Institute on Human Development and Disability at the University of Georgia and the Georgia Council on Developmental Disabilities.

Along the way I managed to recruit Judith Moen and John San Miguel as producers on the project. Their contributions of feedback, time, money, energy, food, directions, favors, and sometimes favors from friends were invaluable to the production and post-production of this project. Simply put there would not be a *Not Home* were it not for the ongoing support and dedication of Judith and John.

Here it is, our labor of love. I hope these personal stories are educational and inspiring.

Introduction

Joe Jowers and I shot the majority of the *Not Home* documentary in HD (High Definition) video using a variety of Canon DSLR cameras. Some interviews are on location, others against black backdrops. We used the Zoom H4N portable audio recorder to capture the sound. This book is the audio transcription of 22 out of more than 80 interviews we conducted across the country over a two year period. I edited each interview for clarity. Although not verbatim, these words are close to the intent and spirit of each person's personal story.

The measure of success for the *Not Home* documentary is somewhat intangible. Of course the number of screenings, film festivals, DVD and book sales, and possible awards are measures of success. But the true success of this project will be measured by how the stories told in the documentary and companion book touch and inspire. There is a parent who feels alone, their back against the wall, and barely hanging on who will get an email, flyer, or phone call to see the documentary or read the book. Afterwards, we hope that parents call their representatives, seek out more support, find a new understanding of the system of institutionalization or perhaps connect with others and embark upon the task of changing the system. This fundamental change is our benchmark for success.

~

Never doubt that a small group of thoughtful committed citizens can change the world; indeed, it's the only thing that ever has.

-Margaret Mead

Chapter One

NICOLE TYSZIEWICZ
ILLINOIS

I have to care for her so much that I'm not able; I'm not engaged in what he's doing. I'm always distracted caring for her that I don't get to participate in his life as a mom should. Kyle is always the one that makes me cry.

My husband and I have been married eleven years and we have three children; we have a six and a half year old, son, his name is Kyle, we have a three and a half year old daughter named McKenna and a newborn daughter who is six months old her name is Kelsey.

This is our child. McKenna.

McKenna is three and half years old and she has primordial dwarfism that means she's very tiny. She is 17 pounds and is actually the same weight as her six month old sister. She has several disabilities; she is blind, has severe scoliosis, hearing deficiency, among...other things. There's a lot. She's severely disabled. She was born premature as well, which caused some issues but right now we're dealing with her needing full time care. She is unfortunately unable to walk or talk, or move independently or do anything independently but she has a wonderful personality and she is a sweetheart to the core.

We're hoping to get sometime soon, some nursing care. We would like to have some nursing care in the home so maybe we could run to the grocery store. My husband and I always have to take turns; it has to usually be one of us. Sometimes we have people that help out for an hour or so but because our daughter has a seizure disorder, we're very nervous about leaving her and people are uncomfortable watching her. And because we're down to one income, we cannot afford to pay a nurse to come in or anybody else who does feel comfortable caring for her. We can't afford to pay anyone to come in either. So we're pretty much stuck at home. I don't wanna say stuck because I love being with McKenna but sometimes you need to get out.

It's a Medical Home Waiver, you need to have that, it's through the state, it's a program through the state, that they would help fund nursing care in the home. Unfortunately, in our state, it's a very long waiting list and I don't know when, how long it'll be. We've been at emergency status for over a year now and have no idea when we'll actually get approved for nursing care.

The waiver would provide a nurse to come to the house and someone who knows about seizure disorders; someone who knows how to give McKenna the medication she needs; knows how to feed her through her feeding tube. I wouldn't have to necessarily be on top of everything, somebody would just be helping me, basically with all her care. They would know how to do everything and be comfortable with it.

Well, as a mother, it would change things for my six year old. That's what always hits me the hardest. He doesn't get to spend a lot of time, quality time, with me or my husband because we're always caring for McKenna and up until recently. The last eight months we've been in the hospital 60 days and we've been bouncing from one crisis to the next, but there's not a lot of the time. We don't get to take Kyle to the park; don't get to take him to the pool or anywhere he wants to go. I can't even… he wants me to be with him at a friend's house on a play date and I can't because we don't necessarily have a place to keep McKenna. I have to care for her so much that I'm not able; I'm not engaged in what he's doing. I'm always distracted caring for her that I don't get to participate in his life as a mom should. Kyle is always the one that makes me cry. I probably should've talked about something else first. This little six year old I tell ya, he's a cool kid. He's a stinker, but he's funny. He's a funny kid. He tries to entertain all the time, which is wonderful, I think he's trying to keep everyone happy and I don't know, it's funny kinda how the instincts kick in even at an early age he's always dressing up and doing different skits and everything to make us laugh so, we try and protect him as much as possible but you know he does live in the same house so he knows what's going on.

Yes, I wouldn't be surprised if he goes into acting.

We do have a support system, a wonderful group of friends and family that help us out. It's a hard place to be to be constantly asking for help and not be able to give anything back. I think that's one of the hardest things I deal with is asking constantly for help. I can't babysit anybody else's kids, I can't go to the grocery store for them, and I don't know when I'll be able to. It's just constantly needing help and can't give back. We do have great friends and what we try and tell ourselves is, they offer, take them up on it once and if they don't wanna help again they won't offer again. But it's, you still feel bad asking. We have a lot of people who come help, kinda mommy's helpers, they're here while I'm here they're helping me but most of my daughter's care needs to be done by me. We have family members who go to the grocery store for us and are happy to babysit for Kyle and Kelsey but not necessarily McKenna which gets hard because we want all three children to be together. We're not separate entities we all come as a package deal so trying figure that out is always a challenge and I understand why people would be afraid to watch McKenna. I do. I get it. She has a seizure disorder; the seizures scare the heck out of me. But we're very thankful for the wonderful people that are in our life and have stuck by us. You know we're going on almost four years now and some people have come and gone, there's a wonderful group that have stayed by us.

Well, it's very difficult for us to take McKenna anywhere. It was funny in late summer, my husband and I took the kids to a park and there were these big tanks there. My son would jump off the tanks and we had a picnic and we did something completely normal and my son kept jumping around saying this is the best day ever. We paid five dollars for parking and we just went to a park but because it was all five of us it was the best day ever for him and McKenna was having a great day and just had fun. We didn't do anything in particular. We didn't have a great meal, probably had peanut butter and jelly but it was a normal day, which we very rarely get. And we don't get to go out much, we really

12

don't. My husband and I, we don't go out for dinner, we don't go out for cocktails we don't. My husband will take Kyle out or I will take Kyle out, it's always separate because McKenna for one reason or another has difficulty going.

The state of Illinois could make it easier for families by making paperwork a little bit easier to fill out by making the process shorter. It's a very lengthy process and then you're just stuck waiting. They just need to make arrangements to have the budget available for families like ours because I don't know how else families are supposed to keep their children at home when it's so difficult without help, all we need is the little bit of help.

If I had a chance to talk to the governor, I would tell him to make this a priority because my daughter needs to be home with me, with her family, but we do need a certain amount of help; we need a little bit of help to get us through the day, somebody that's capable which would be a nurse, and that does get expensive but it certainly doesn't cost as much as a child being put in a home or a residential facility. We want our daughter at home and all we want is a little bit of help. And the money's there, they just need to find a way to make it work.

Well, I know about several facilities in the area, in the Chicagoland area. They've been brought up to us since my daughter's been born; that it just might be easier to put your daughter in a home. And I certainly respect the people that do that, that understand that they cannot provide the care that they need. But my daughter needs to be home with me. She's my daughter and I need to care for her but I need a little help.

Governor Quinn, the State of Illinois and all the decision makers, I am asking for a budget to be set aside for helping families with children with severe developmental disabilities. We need help in our homes, the children are meant to be at home and we can care for them well, we do need help though, a lot of help. I would appreciate you coming into our home, spending some time with us and seeing the beauty of our family together but also seeing how difficult it can be day after day after day caring for our special little girl.

Help! Please! Just find a way to help, honestly, plain and simple.

Our daughter, McKenna has certainly taught us patience and she has restored our faith in humanity. We have wonderful people in our lives, we've had strangers come into our lives trying to help us in ways that they can; cooking us a meal, sending a kind note. She's inspiring. I guess before she was born I never would've thought how a child that couldn't talk or walk could inspire. She does, every single day; she's a beautiful spirit and beautiful personality and a wonderful part of our family.

Chapter Two

KIMBALL HUMPHREYS
COLUMBIA, MO

The medical people said, "You need to go to the grief counselors because your son's not going home. He is going to die tonight."

My ex-wife was very excited about having a child. She comes from a large Roman Catholic background where there are lots of children. I was adopted. I had one brother so I wasn't really big on huge families. She wanted to have babies so when she became pregnant she did it all right. She got away from any kind of alcohol and any other kind of stimulants like caffeine. She took all the right vitamins. She was thinking that she's gonna get married, she's gonna have babies, and everything is going to be tough for a while and then you sit back and relax, and everything is fine. That's the life her siblings had, the life her parents had and the life most people have but... That just didn't happen for her.

Brock was born normal full term birth. At three days of age that night he went into a coma. The medical people said, "You need to go to the grief counselors because your son's not going home. He is going to die tonight."

So it was really, really tragic to her—it was to me too, I can't deny that. So it was out of the blue, didn't anticipate anything like this happening. Found out that Brock had a metabolic disorder that was undiagnosed. They didn't test for that at birth; they do now in the state of Missouri to prevent this sort of thing. That coma caused brain swelling, no speech for Brock, gross motor skills deficiencies and fine motor skill deficiencies. He woke up after two weeks. We took Brock home after three weeks. That next day we took him back. He had another issue so I've had him hospitalized over 12 or 13 times. It put a lot of strain, a lot of stress on the marriage. We did our best. We did get a huge amount of help from our families. They were a little bit nervous about what they could do couldn't do. They knew how sick Brock was and knew that we were the most attuned to what his needs were so they helped where they could. But she became overwhelmed and obsessed that he was special needs, to the point where she used other methods of dealing with the stress to kind of avoid it. She drank a lot of alcohol. It just got her. It's just one of those things where you deal with it the best you can and it gets depressing for some people, and they just can't handle it.

On the other hand, I'm pretty well tuned into it. I changed my thought process and my outlook on life was different. I realized Brock was here for a reason. Part of that reason is that we can help others down the road get better services, hopefully.

It is difficult. It's difficult, and I try to tell people about this. I've spoken to lunch groups, and normally the first few years I did well. But a couple of years ago I'd break out in tears. I'd ball my eyes out in front of these people and only be able to talk about three or four minutes. I've since then adjusted how I look at this, and I try and look at it from the perspective of helping people. It's an awareness issue. A lot of people used to hide their kids that are special needs. I don't care who looks at us. I don't care what they say. He's here, I'm here, and we are going to make the best of our lives. He and I hang out a lot together. He doesn't have buddies that come over and play baseball or basketball or anything. It's basically me and Brock and his sister. Brock visits with his mom a couple of nights a week, which I think is very important.

Brock is 16 now, just turned 16 last week, and he's doing well, he's a fun kid. He can't communicate well, but he does sign and he has an augmentative speech device that he can use, too.

Brock's on several medications so he takes a couple of meds in the morning and then a couple at night. We have to be very; very cautious that we keep track of what he eats and keep him away from things he can't eat. His problem is with ammonia levels. If his ammonia levels spike, it will put him in a coma. I have to mix his formula up every morning. That's six different dry products I weigh out on gram scales that's gotta be made fresh everyday. Brock drinks that throughout the day and he cannot eat a lot of protein so we have to keep track of every gram of protein. He can not eat meat or peanut butter or nuts or cheese or dairy products. So we have to be cautious when he changes schools. Whenever we travel we have to be careful about having all these powders and gram scales, so we usually carry a letter from his doctor. I think his body can absorb that a little better now so he's not so prone to being hospitalized if he gets a stomach flu.

We get our services mainly through Boone County Family Resources. We get respite care. They help us with things like therapeutic writing or special baseball league that Brock plays in the challenger league. They help fund those kind of things because everything is expensive especially medications. They help us with that. They help us with physical therapy, speech therapy, occupational therapy, with inserts in his shoes, with augmentative communication devices. They have helped us all along the way, and they helped get us on the Medicaid Waiver list so that Medicaid can kick in and help pay for some of Brock's issues. Boone County Family Resources is very creative in getting funding of all these issues. Especially the waiver, that's the big issue.

If they were not helping me I'm not certain where we'd be... I suppose he'd be gone; he'd be gone totally. I think he'd have not made it through the first six or seven years of life as sick as he was.

I know the only other option you have is to spend down all your money, your income, and all your possessions and I think you have to get below a thousand dollars and then they'll help care for Brock. So it becomes a question of you either turn him over to the state and let them care for him and worry about his care and his survival percentage because as many times as he was hospitalized that's a big issue.

I was always there to make sure he got his medications on time. So I think it's hard to envision what it would be like without help.

The stress will do you in if you're not careful.

The finances of doing something like raising a special needs child it's overwhelming. I thought I could handle it initially and I spent all my

17

money and I spent all my saving and spent more money than I had, and I ended up with financial problems that I took the blame for and I kept my ex-wife out of it, but I think that just overwhelmed her. My personality is a little different. I just take it one step at a time; like eating an elephant one bite at a time.

My ex-wife just seemed to dwell on the fact that her life was so horrible and that I think it kind of sneaked up on us. I think that it was probably five or six years ago. I think sometimes at that point it was like a mid-life crises maybe. It seemed like she entered into and her mid-life crisis coupled with Brock and his issues. That just overwhelmed her. And she didn't know how to deal with it. I think that she was confused and unable to admit that you need help sometimes from professionals. I'm not afraid to admit that. It was just starting to make the turn, and she was wanting to have more fun herself. Which is nothing wrong with that but that's not what we can do in our life. Our fun has to be a different kind of fun; it has to be focused on the children and not on ourselves and our own wants.

I determined that the four of us living together, I have a younger daughter 13, the four of us living together just wasn't going to work. I had hoped that if I initiated a divorce and filed for divorce it would shock my wife into realizing she needed to make some changes in her patterns of behavior, and if she did make those changes she'd have a lot more time with her children and specifically helping out with Brock's growth. But as it turns out I think she's happier because now Brock's there a couple of days a week and she can deal with that. He goes over there after school for just about an hour or two, and I think that's just about right. Had we maybe had a nanny or if we were rich enough to have someone to care for Brock she would have been fine with the whole situation from the first, but that's not our life. So it worked out well. I'm happier. She's happier. I think the children are both happier. So it's okay. The kids are getting enough of mom, and they get lots of dad so it works out well.

Attention is a very big issue. The attention that Brock's sister gets or her feelings about that attention sometimes overwhelm her. She wants it.

18

She's 13 so all these years growing up with a brother that is three years older but acts younger, or seems younger. This has been a little difficult for her. I think when she was younger up through about 10 or 11 she did great. We didn't ask her to do too much, but as she got older we probably asked her for a little more help than we should have. And it seemed we were giving Brock more attention; it was specifically medical attention. So she felt a need for more attention as she approached becoming a teenager. Now I think that it's working well because her brother spends some alone time with mom and during that time she can have alone time with me and vice versa. She can spend some alone time with her mom. It's not that she wants to avoid her brother, but now she gets some one on one time with each of us. That's very good quality time. She's very good with her brother she signs with him, plays with him some, but she has her life too. As we all know, as children get older they tend to gravitate to their peer group and spend more time with them that's understandable. She's a wonderful little girl and very well, very well balanced for such a young child. She's really tuned in to kids with special needs. If she has one in a class where someone's a little bit slower she tunes in and becomes aware of that a little quicker. She is more sensitive to their needs.

Try your hardest to find some way to keep your child at home with you. If you need round the clock medical care try and find resources to help. It is tough to find resources as a parent because we don't know the acronyms or the names, and you go on a web site and you might just get totally lost with everything but if you can, find an agency or a state agency that will sometimes direct you to someone that can help. Anything you can do to keep your child with you other than putting them in a home or a facility. And I think that can make you a much better person. If you didn't start out a good person, you are going to be even better. I don't know what I would do without Brock. It'd certainly be easier and I could be selfish and go do what I want to do, but that's just not as important to me anymore. I think it's much more important to do things with him and to share with him.

I think that it's a good opportunity to speak about what's inside of me because of Brock. When you have a child with special needs it gives you a lot more time to sit and think. When you're at the hospital sitting and thinking or at a doctor's appointment or some other kind of medical problem with Brock. At the school waiting to meet with the special needs teachers or the IEP meeting, it gives you a little time to think about what's going on. Think about how important it is that he or she is in your life. How much you can do for them. How much they depend on you. I think even kids that are unable to move anything but their eyes or their mouth they can paint beautiful pictures or tell beautiful stories. It's just a question of sitting and enjoying that. But I'm the type, I'm full, I'm full of Jesus. I love life, and I love my life every day. It's always wonderful. I don't care if it's raining, or it's sunny every day is a wonderful day. It's a beautiful world, and we're not here very long. We may as well enjoy whatever we have whatever we can take with us in our mind, and that's really all I have to say...

Chapter Three

LAURA & ONIEDA HURSE
KANSAS CITY, MO

Don't give up! You never know what your child can do unless you push 'em. Don't give up! Don't give up on your child. You gave birth to that child. Don't give up on that child.

Laura: I was in denial in my disability group for a long time. But it took me a while to like, accept my disability for the most part, because in elementary school I was really mainstream, which means I went to a lot of regular classes except for math and gym. Obviously, I couldn't do the physical stuff that everyone else did when it came to gym. In math, I'm still not good at math, but I've been pretty much mainstream my whole life.

Onieda: Well, you know, as her mom, when she first started school there the school district that I worked in and they were at one point moving a lot of kids in wheelchairs to one particular building. We went over to the district to have her tested at St. Lukes so that I would know where her grade level would be. Would she be normal, high functional, or whatever? So she was normal. She was where she was supposed to be. So the push was to put her in a mainstream regular classroom. Mentally she's fine. She has a physical disability, so that was a big issue for me to make sure she was put with normal kids so she could learn. And that has been a big push.

Onieda: She just always wanted to be a part of everything. So you have to learn how to handle yourself in a regular population and so that helps. She was in Girl Scouts. She always tease me, because she went to Girl Scout camp. How many, eight years?

Laura: Yeah, eight years in a row, and my brother went to camp.

Onieda: Eight years. You sent your handicap daughter to camp, but didn't send your son to day camp, OK! But that's just the way it was, because I wanted her to be independent. So that she won't be so dependent. It was important for her to feel good about herself. So not to be so dependent on her mom, so, one day I will die, and she's gonna have to be able to stand on her own.

Onieda: Me being a single parent at that point, I worked with my kids. We did Hooked On Phonics and the whole ten yards for both of them to make sure they were able to read, because you know, reading is very important so I made sure they were able to do those things.

Onieda: Really, my sisters and everybody lived in St. Louis and so it was just me and the kids. I can say that I had a child care center person or a home day care provider who was really my right-arm a lot of the time. I've always worked. By profession, I'm a teacher, and I work for the School District of Kansas City Missouri. I have a Masters. I like teaching. I've always done early childhood and so that's always been my thing. I've always taught or did non-profit work in early childhood. So she was always out in Onieda: Hickermills district where she went to school, and if they got sick; either one of them got sick Ms. Allen would go get them. You have to have somebody who can kind of help you out, so she was that person. I'd say Ms. Allen can you go get him and take him to your house until I was able to get off work? Really, she was my backbone.

Onieda: When they were little, they had another home provider. I was blessed - I must have did right by somebody else's children - because I was blessed to have other people to come in and kind of help me with that.

Onieda: So I've been blessed. I really have been blessed with some good support. Because overall, it was just me and the kids.

Onieda: My sister came and got them for the summer and took them to St. Louis. They were included in all the family functions and interacting with cousins. They were surrounded by positive people. I would say. Really good people to help you get through whatever.

Laura: High School... Oh gosh! I hated high school so bad. I was really, really, really, struggling with coming to terms with the fact that I had a disability, because I used to get picked on all the time, everyday. From the time I was a freshman until the 2nd part of my junior year; spring semester of my junior year, I hated it that much. I would cry everyday for four years of my life, 'cause I hated going to school every day, because they would make fun of me so bad.

Onieda: There were some positive things in some of those episodes that happened in high school. The good Lord always sent her somebody to befriend her. In the midst of all that she was going through, there was a couple of people who came through and befriended her, so that helped her get through some of those rough periods at that time. Because you know, in that development age they're struggling with who they are anyway. So, there was a couple of people who came by and said, "Come on Laura, we're gonna do this." Melissa in particular bringing movies to the house, and brownies, and come to the house and visiting with her.

Laura: But I did do well. I got a scholarship to go to college. I volunteered. I tutored elementary school kids in reading and stuff, so, yeah. I got a scholarship to go to school.

I graduated a semester earlier because I hated high school so much.

Laura: Oh there was no quitting. No, no quitting. I would not quit because I knew what I wanted to do with my life. Because, I've always known I wanted to be an attorney, I just didn't know what type of attorney. I always tell my mom that I really didn't want to be like, put in one box of being a disability attorney. I just come to the conclusion that that is who I am. It doesn't define who I am, but it's a part of who I am so I just might as well accept it and move on with it, and just go with what I know.

Laura: I never got along with people with disabilities in high school as much as I got along with mainstream counselors because I thought I was different from them, but I wasn't. I was not used to being alone with other people with disabilities. So like, after high school, I didn't accept myself, because I didn't ever want to be excluded from anything.

Laura: I think it's all been really beneficial to me because I learned how to interact with a lot of people; I learned I could go to college and to do well. I don't know where I would be if I would have stayed in Special-Ed classes all my life.

Laura: Now I'm a student at the University Missouri Kansas City. Community college was a big difference because I really started to find my voice there. That's where I really, really, really started to find my voice and I started interacting with more people with disabilities. I eventually got to the point where I became a tutor for people with disabilities in the political science department and I got paid for it.

Laura: I guess they thought that I knew what I knew well enough that they entrusted me to do that job for a semester. And then I became a student ambassador there and they let me give tours and stuff of the campus to new and incoming freshmen, high school students, and non-disability and disability students, and so I got to be a good voice for people with disabilities on campus.

Onieda: As a parent I really didn't think about it as being hard. Because people always say, "Well, we need to figure out..." what is there to figure out, you do what you got to do and move on. 'Cause if you sit and think about it, you are gonna start feeling like, "Oh, whoa is me", but I didn't have time to think about "Oh, whoa is me". I just had to do what I had to do and make sure that they were well taken care of.

Onieda: Then when she went into community college, that's when, like she said, she began to have more of a voice and then she saw more.

Onieda: You gotta push and it's always got to be constant. You gotta encourage your child.

Onieda: You gonna have problems with people anyway, you gonna have problems because one thing you're a minority, and then you're a minority in a wheelchair so you got two faces on it, but that's ok, you got to get through it. You gotta move on, get through it and keep on because it will pass. All those things will pass.

Laura: Yeah! I never really thought about it like that until recent years. It just clicked in me one day and it went "OK come to terms with who you are", "It's ok to be you, you know". Because you really don't

24

have to deal with these people everyday like you did in high school or regular school, because you don't have to hear them if you don't want to.

Laura: Because in high school nobody was like me. I always knew I wanted to go to college. There was nobody like me that I could identify with until I got into college.

Oneida: I want her to eventually find her own place, because I'm gonna die one day and I want to know that she gonna be ok. I know she can speak up for herself and I know all those good things, but I want to see her out to do her own life, because, I want to see that before something ever happens to me, because she's capable of doing it. We can't necessarily depend on family. It's something that she's gotta do for herself.

Laura: I want to move out...

Oneida: Yeah, she wanna leave me!

Laura: ...move to a different state.

Oneida: She wanna leave her momma!

Laura: I really do want to move to like Washington, DC, or to Texas because, like soon, after I graduate I want to be gone out of here so bad.

Oneida: No! Nobody ever encouraged me to send her to an institution. Nobody did. When people, when children are born with a disability, you get all kinds of reactions. You, yourself as a parent you're going to feel like; "what did I do wrong, and blah, blah?" You feel and go through all this guilt and all those things, and then people will say things to you like, "Well is she retarded? Is she this? Is she that?" And you struggle with that but then you have to come to grips with who you are in your child...

Onieda: This is my child. I was 30 plus years old, so it's my baby and so I was gonna keep my baby. So I was gonna do whatever I needed to do, and at the time I wanted a baby.

Onieda: In preparation for this in my mind, in hindsight; I've always taken Special-Ed classes; I've worked with kids with different abilities and non-abilities, so I feel that maybe this is what God planned all along for me to have...I was gonna have a child with disabilities, and so when

25

she came along that's who I had, and so I took care of my baby, and so there was no options.

Onieda: I knew what to do with her; I knew to put her on the floor, and make her do things for herself. I knew to try to even though they said she's not gonna be able to eat on her own. And with all the surgeries and stuff that she's had, we've gone through 'em, with God, and we had to go through it to get where we are today. Sometimes it make you strong, and I think it just depends on you as a parent, because we've seen other kids that grew up with her in those situations, in the same school setting; some parents were very motivating and some were not.

Onieda: Laura was born early. She was born with CP. She was like 28 weeks early; premature baby and she's spent a month and a half, basically in ICU, in a NIC unit when she was born. She was real little, like 10.5 inches long; 2lbs, 2oz. So she looked like a little hairy rat at the time and so she grew. So she's very confident now and at this point, that confidence didn't come easy for Laura, but I've always encouraged her to do things for herself and to kind of think for herself.

Onieda: I believe that everybody can contribute to society in their own way, but they have to be given the opportunity. I don't think that people who live in institutions are given opportunities like we are, like people who don't live in an institution, which is really unfair because they have a voice too. And that's why I'm so vocal about disability rights because I know who I represent. I represent people who can't speak up for themselves.

Onieda: We had to advocate a lot! I had to advocate a lot for services for Laura. I had to speak up and tell 'em what I wanted and what I didn't want. We had to call the House of Representatives when things didn't go well, we said, this has to stop, and sent letters to get things accomplished. To get a wheelchair; just to get a wheelchair, we had to write a letter 'cause the healthcare wasn't gonna pay for it.

Onieda: from, it's just you have to do it. You gotta speak up; don't sit back and let it go by, you have to speak up.

Onieda: Don't give up! You never know what your child can do unless you push 'em. Don't give up! Don't give up on your child. You gave birth to that child. Don't give up on that child.

Onieda: I think that people with a disability should have the same rights as everybody else in America. They're American citizens too!

Chapter Four

TONI AND JAMES HOY
ILLINOIS

And we were forced to choose between an irresponsible thing which
would be to bring him home and an illegal thing, which would
be to leave him at the hospital and in doing so we were
charged with neglect, we were indicted for neglect.

Daniel is 16 years old. He is currently at Chaddock Residential Treatment Center in Quincy Illinois where he has been since May. Prior to that he was at Streamwood Behavioral Health Center for two years. He is diagnosed with post-traumatic stress disorder and obsessive-compulsive disorder due to pre-adoptive neglect and trauma. TONI: He was prenatally affected by alcohol and drugs and he has a severe anxiety disorder which causes him to be extremely aggressive and violent hurting people and damaging property.

JAMES: With multiple hospital stays, Danny, we felt that for the safety of our family, ourselves and our other three children that we had to leave Danny in the hospital. And to do that we knew that we would be charged with a lockout. And it comes down to that we neglected out child.

TONI: The therapist recommended residential treatment for him. We were not able to access that treatment using our funds or any state funds; we were turned down for everything. And we were forced to choose between an irresponsible thing which would be to bring him home and an illegal thing, which would be to leave him at the hospital and in doing so we were charged with neglect, we were indicated for neglect. The state put our name on the state central register for child abusers.

28

TONI: He was two years old when he came to live with us as a foster child and we adopted him two years later.

TONI: Daniel is in the only trauma treatment center in the state of Illinois. It's a facility with about six or eight cottages. There are ten boys in his cottage all with mental illness and behavioral issues, emotional issues and there is a staff of, one staff to two clients. He gets round the clock therapy and care. There's a school on the facility.

JAMES: Department of Children and Family Service, who places the children there have five beds and we know of at least six to eight to 10 couples that have children that need mental health services. We know of ten people the Department of Children and Family Services has to know of a lot more. And we [the state of Illinois] has five beds. That is a problem. This is the only trauma treatment center in the state of Illinois and is one of two that my wife and I know of in the whole Midwest.

TONI:Even if there were more available, more trauma treatment centers there's still the issue of access to the centers and funding for it. It's very expensive, it's $150,000 dollars a year and insurance does not cover it at all. For adoptive children who are domestic adoptions, they all—if it's a special needs adoption they have an adoption subsidy. And that subsidy will help us with outpatient therapies but it does not include residential treatment. There's a hard line where it will not cover any portion of the residential treatment so that expense falls completely on the parents and when we can't afford it that's where we get caught in the Catch 22 where we're forced to choose between treatment and custody.

TONI:Governor Quinn, the Medicaid law, there is a provision in the Medicaid Law called the EPSDT Early Pre-diagnostic Screening and Treatment and that provision says that if a practitioner of the healing arts deems that a treatment is medically necessary to correct or ameliorate a condition the state must provide it. If the state does not provide it they must arrange for it. All adoptive children that are adopted through special needs adoption have Medicaid and if Illinois was following the federal Medicaid law for these very traumatized children when we get to a point where they need residential treatment because it's recommended by a therapist their Medicaid cards should cover that treatment. And the

29

reason that it's not happening is because the behavioral health centers are not licensed as psychiatric residential treatment facilities. And if they were licensed properly we could call the center and get our children admitted Medicaid would cover and we wouldn't lose custody.

JAMES: Along those same lines though, they've known for over 20 years that this was a problem. If your child has an alcohol problem, or was a criminal with mental health problem he could get services and we wouldn't lose our custody rights. So I mean it's taken them twenty years and they've done nothing. I mean that is the real frustrating part about the whole... problem.

TONI:If a child has mental and behavioral health issues alone we have to trade custody rights for mental health care. If a child has mental and behavioral issues concurrent with drug abuse issues the child gets treatment but the parents retain custody.

Read more of Toni Hoy's story in her book:

Second Time Foster Child: How One Family Adopted a Fight Against the State for their Son's Mental Healthcare while Preserving their Family – Available at www.secondtimefosterchild.com/

Chapter Five

ERIC CARLSON
ILLINOIS

The common theme with all the parents, all of the kids were born drug exposed early on and DCFS says to us, yes they were born drug exposed but all they need is a little love and attention and they'll be okay.

Joshua is 16 years old and he is currently in Steamwood Behavioral Mental Health Facility trying to get his medication stabilized so he can return to his residential treatment facility.

My wife and I went to court earlier this week to answer allegations of neglect and abuse as a result of the psychological lockout that occurred...as a result of our son's condition. Specifically neglect. We were charged with neglect and abuse. It's simply as a result of locking out. There's no other explanation that's provided in the court documents or the charges, just neglect and abuse. And the only thing the state's attorney has to prove in the case is that we went through the act of locking him out. Our son, he became like a light switch. One day he was—he's always been difficult over the years to keep in line with school and behavioral but we managed. We had therapy and counseling and medication. Somewhere along the line he was advised of his rights and he no longer needed to take medicine after the age of twelve. So once he found that out it became difficult to keep him medicated and stable which led to odd and erratic behaviors like jumping out of windows at night and going and finding drugs and alcohol and trying to run away. So there was probably seven police involvements and the last involvement he alcohol poisoned himself and while he was at the hospital and they wouldn't admit him to the psychiatric unit, we proceeded with the lock out to get him the help he needed.

Today we met with state Senator Susan Garret out of Highland Park Illinois and through the efforts of Tony and Jim Hoy they were able to publicize this problem that all of these parents that really didn't know that other parents are going through. We all feel alone and that there's no one else doing anything like what we're going through. But through Toni Hoy's efforts putting together a website sharing their story we were linked up and we found them. I was trying to sort through our own personal problems with our situation and come to find out that there's probably dozens of other families that were looking for the same sort of help. So Toni Hoy through her efforts contacted Susan Garret. She agreed to meet with us because she couldn't believe what she was hearing of the problems that all these families were enduring and she was confused as to how could this be. So there were three families that met directly with her today and probably four to six that dialed in via conference call to explain their stories to the senator.

The common theme with all these parents is that all of the kids were born drug exposed early on and DCFS says to us, yes they were born drug exposed but all they need is a little love and attention and they'll be okay. And often that is the case for the early years of the children's life but as they develop mentally and physically some of them take a turn for the worse. We adopted two children, biological half brothers, and one has had no problems and then we have this other son that has the problems.

The source of the problem, as we see it, is that families are made aware, through the DCFS system, of all kinds of services that are available. These are post-adoption services and to take advantage of them but it's a very complicated system to navigate. Even if you're an expert, it's difficult.

In our case we knew nothing of any of these services. When we adopted our kids they were just a normal part of our lives. We raised them, took them to therapy, did what we had to do and didn't know any services existed. By the time our child really degraded and we started to discover some of these services that were out there but they were very difficult to get, they were hard to navigate. They were hard to get. It was a long drawn out process and we didn't have that kind of time. And our son started to engage in activities that were higher risk and he needed immediate intervention and that wasn't available to people in crisis. So that the only way that our son could get the help is through the process of a lock out because immediately once your child is a ward of the state they have to treat that child for whatever is the problem. As parents we don't have the same luxury unless we had the money that it takes to treat them ourselves and that's at least $150,000 dollars per year to have residential treatment for your children. So, on one hand, a little love is all we need for the children is how they are handed to us and then when the problems really hit the fan as they grow older when we need those services; it's not something you can handle on your own.

Joshua and his brother Zachery came into our life at 18 months and three years. Joshua is the younger one at 18 months. They were, had already been bounced around in two or three other foster homes prior to us getting them at 18 months and three years. So they went through their own little trauma at that point.

Joshua is our son that is having problems now but he has a half brother Zachery. And we took both Zachery and Joshua into our home when Joshua was 18 months and Zachery was three years. They had already been in foster care in 2 or 3 homes prior to us getting them. They were adopted perhaps between two or three years after foster care because the state requires that there's permanency for the child that after a certain point in their life they have to be placed somewhere permanent. So our children…originally we were truly foster parents and they were going to be returned to their original birth mother who had drug issues and when she achieved her goals and when she achieved her goals with DCFS these children would be returned to them. That never happened so her rights were terminated as an adult, and as a parent. So we need either to adopt the children or they need to be placed in another foster home. So at that point we adopted them.

The baddest of the bad, there a big list of bad that but probably the thing he's in most jeopardy of is probably the gang initiation to the Gangster Disciples. He committed arson and lit a car on fire underneath the bedroom window of some children that were sleeping up above. They weren't hurt but it is definitely a very serious crime. And that all occurred, all of his criminal behaviors occurred once he left our custody and got into the DCFS custody. In our opinion a big part of the problem with all of this is that they want us to parent the children, they want us to take responsibility for raising the children but when they get them the focus is the will of the child. As a normal teenager without any mental health history he has problems processing what reality is. They have their own will that often conflicts with how the parents are trying to raise them. So when he got into the system they would say you are going to this residential or this group home. You are not allowed to leave. If you leave we will call the police. Well, there's no consequences. They call the police the child comes back to the home and he continues to make defiance but he's integrating with criminal elements out in the community. He enjoyed that. He thought that he was being a gangster and that this was the life that he wanted to lead. So his criminal path, he had five arrests within a two-month period and all things that are going to make his future uncertain.

Currently he's at a mental hospital called Streamwood Behavioral Health Facility. And he's there because he was kicked out of the residential treatment home that he was staying at due to his hostile and aggressive behavior. By being in the residential facility it gives him intensive therapy. They have group therapy everyday he gets his education, he's off the streets, safe. So our hope is that he will be able to get out of the mentally health facilities and get to the residential facility so that he can continue to heal and deprogram his criminal and gangster ways that he's embraced.

34

Chapter Six

DEMMI ECKLOFF
BIRMINGHAM, AL

My college experience has so far exceeded my expectations and the people here have really embraced me.

My name is Demmi Eckloff and I am a freshman at Samford University in Birmingham, Alabama.

My college experience has so far exceeded my expectations and the people here have really embraced me. So here I am. It has worked with me so well. It's fun. I have a note taker so she takes my notes for me. I have some accommodations but other than that I'm in typical classes that we have to take as freshmen and I'm in there with typical students.

I'm definitely a people person. I know whatever I do I can't work in a cubicle I have to be one on one working with people. I'm not really sure, I thought about psychology... maybe going the counselor route. I'm trying to stay open minded and just figure it out.

I'm a ward of the state so they dictate where I can and where I can't be. According to them I should be at home for my entire life or be in a nursing home. I want to be as typical as possible and college was the next step for me.

Medicaid would like to see me at home. They have threatened me in the past to place me in a nursing home, but my parents weren't going to allow that. So I have to decide what I want to do with my life.

My mom is very feisty, to say the least. And we were in a meeting with some of the head people in Medicaid and they said if you can't take care of her and you don't want her just put her in the nursing home.

Let's say that I can't remember it much because I was in utter shock...utter shock. Thinking about it makes me sad. Yes, I have a disability but everyone else embraces me for who I am, so they should too. And I'm smart enough to make my own decisions so they should let me.

I was born with a form of congenital muscular dystrophy. It affects all the muscles besides my heart. Mostly my diaphragm so an ordinary cold for me is at least a two week bed stay. Where I can't get out of bed. Possibly a hospital stay. I can't raise my arms up, I can't lift my legs. So I have to have help. Everyone has to do everything for me. But I do not mean that in a mean sense. But I do dictate what I need and advocate for myself.

Yeah, sometimes too clearly maybe.

Growing up my family never saw the disability. I was in a small community; for the most part they did not see the disability. I did typical things; I was in ballet as a little kid. Soccer, softball... all that fun stuff. The school system treated me as all typical classes and I had accommodations as needed. I was very fortunate and everyone embraced me. I have had you know, ups and downs of sicknesses. You know, I ask why do I have muscular dystrophy but for the most part I try to stay upbeat and I think that is why I have had such a fortunate life.

I had good grades but my mom truly got me here I feel. She saw my dream and determination.

My mom is feisty. I think that helps the situation I am in. I made good grades and I think she saw my determination that I wanted to get here, and my dream my mom truly made it possible. She helped through this whole process, working with Medicaid. She's hired a lawyer she's up at night sending emails this whole past year and more. She's truly my hero.

If I were in a nursing home right now I don't think I would live as long of a life cause I would get so depressed and probably die. I just feel so sorry for the kids that are already in there. I would just want to try and help them have a typical life and move out on their own. I know for sure that the attendants at the nursing home I would drive them crazy. I am pampered and I would be telling them to paint my finger nails, turn the

TV channel and I don't know if they would be that attentive and I would drive myself silly.

What would I say to a parent that's in the position of putting their child in a nursing home? And I would say although you are in a jam try and see your child's full potential and if you think that's where they should be, in a nursing home, fine. But I don't think that any child with a disability unless that is her dream, which I can't imagine person's dream to live in a nursing home. I would ask the child what their dream is. Consider it. Try to make it happen and you really have to fight the system. The states are not nice about it. They see us as, I feel like a piece of trash. But I think the more we fight, we bring that to the states and show them that we have the same feelings as others, hopefully they will understand in time. I would just tell the parent consider the child's dream. And how can you make that possible.

I love it here but Medicaid will only give me 50 hours a week for nursing hours, so that means that I only get to stay on campus four nights. And I am pissed I want to be here just like everybody else seven days a week, seven nights. Especially activities but my mom has to drive me back and forth. But then fortunately I live close but I am truly upset. And they need to know it. And they refuse to meet me. And I feel that they are treating me like trash. And if they met me they'd change their decision.

Chapter Seven

KIM ECKLOFF
BIRMINGHAM, AL

When the states realize they can save money by keeping the person in the environment they want, the community setting, we will all be better. We will be more compassionate people. We will have a greater understanding of humanity and we will do what's right.

I'm Kim Eckloff and I live in Birmingham, Alabama. I'm the mother of three daughters, Austin, Demi and Anislee and right now we are on the Samford University campus where Demi is a freshman.

Samford University has been in session about 4 weeks so she started about 5 weeks ago and we had the privilege to move in about a week prior to get everything adjusted. Demi has always been an outgoing and charismatic person but I have seen her really become outgoing living in a dorm situation. When I come to visit her she's always got people in her room or she's in their room. And she's had a great relationship with her professors none of which I've orchestrated or been involved with. She just seems to have embraced this campus and the campus has really taken to her. I will say that this has been the longest period she has been without illness. We have not been hospitalized and she has not been sick in a long period and I really think it's because she's in a good mental state of mind here.

So one of the greatest obstructions is because she uses a ventilator about twelve hours a day and she receives Medicaid nursing for those hours. The Medicaid agency as a whole has limited her time that she can get nursing hours to 50 hours a week. Subsequently she has to be in the home the remaining hours of the week. So she has to be home Friday, Saturday and Sunday and I have to check in twice a day at 6 am and 6 pm to sign the nurse in and the nurse out. So that's one of the greatest obstructions. The state law is written that the person should remain in the home. But first we had the hurdle recognizing that this was going to be Demi's new home the dorm room. The state didn't want to recognize her dorm as her home. We got over that hurdle.

And then they don't want to recognize that she is capable of signing in her attendant for the day which her father and I pay for so I have to come over and sign the Medicaid nurse out every morning then relinquish her help to her attendant during the day.

I understand that the laws were written so long ago and they are that the laws were written to protect the people as a whole; however I want to individualize that for Demi. I don't believe that this is the right environment and truthfully this is not what I saw for Demi. We built our house with a full apartment for Demi and attendant care. I never really envisioned her living away at college. I thought she'd do online course work and live in our home with attendant care. But, this is her decision. She said she wanted to go to college "just like my sister went to college this is what you and my father did and this is what I want to do. This is what's typical." And so I supported that decision. I said how can we make this happen? I have had to have quite a bit of legal representation to make this happen and at this point we really do not have an agreement with the state that this is ok. It's just a temporary situation that we know could end at anytime.

Demi was born with congenital Muscular Dystrophy and a very rare form at that Merosin deficiency. In a typical pregnancy it's a recessive trait, it's very rare. However we knew at about six weeks when she wasn't developing correctly and at 8 months she was in a wheelchair and motorized wheelchair at 18 months. However we knew she was cognitive typical because she took to driving her wheelchair immediately and she was making all the other cognitive milestones typically. In fact probably ahead, she spelled her name real early although her talking came late. She didn't sit up roll over any of those milestones. For the most part we knew she was cognitively typical but physically disabled.

We never heard that she should be institutionalized. She was born in Wisconsin. We never heard that she should be institutionalized at her birth. However, through the years, many physicians have suggested that they thought she would die just because they thought her muscles would quote unquote burnout. However, in recent years the state of Alabama has challenged me on a couple times. One time, a couple years ago, they came into our home and said that because of her severe need if we ever felt that we couldn't take care of her that she would have to be institutionalized. I've always felt that I can take care of her. However, I have asked for support from the state. We never had night nursing before two and a half years ago. I turned Demi every 15 to 20 minutes as she asked and I did the ventilator and I did the feeding too. So the intensive care didn't allow me to work, it didn't allow me to go to college it didn't allow any me to further any of my personal goals. So when I asked the state of Alabama for support and they continued to deny it and said maybe I should consider institution. And as of recent when I have said that she'll be going to college and living in a dormitory room with attendant and nursing care they suggested that if I couldn't take care of her that she needed to be in an institution. And at that time I said correction, living in a dorm and an institution are clearly different and I can take care of her but this is her choice.

I can't always answer how I feel when I talk to the state of Alabama without evoking a lot of emotion. Because I want Demi to realize her dreams. Those are her dreams those aren't my dreams. So when I hear people on the other end of the phone, particularly Commissioner Steckel say to me when she's not willing to meet us in person and to really know and understand who Demi is. When I hear her say that I can't care for my child and she belongs in an institution. She has no way to understand as a parent how difficult it is for me when I just want what Demi wants. She just wants her education just like her sister had just like any other person. So that particular conversation was particularly igniting. I got extremely feisty on the other end of the conversation because that was my initial reaction and probably I was inappropriate in talking to Commissioner Steckel. It's not that I'm so insulted personally. I see the state of

Alabama stepping in the way of Demi's dreams and I just want her to have access to the same opportunities that my other two children have or that I have or that any other 18 year old has. That's why I have remained feisty. I heard Demi use that word and that's why I have remained feisty.

If I were approached by a parent considering putting their child in a nursing home, I would hold that parent's hand and ask them is that their decision or their child's decision? I personally would try and work with them to see what other options are available. There are community resources, there are community supports and it is a lot cheaper to keep your children and adults in a community setting than it is in a nursing home. When the states realize they can save money by keeping the person in the environment they want, the community setting, we will all be better. We will be more compassionate people. We will have a greater understanding of humanity and we will do what's right. So I would ask a parent if that is their decision and why, and if there is a way that we can troubleshoot what resources were available and support mechanisms for them. It's just a matter of time and we can appeal to different family support groups but there's no one center that demonstrates what resources are available. So that's very hard. I have had to work as a full-time job to get the necessary community resources for Demi and I do have the luxury of not having to work. My husband provides for us. So I understand that if a parent has to do that that is a very hard decision and I am glad that is not my decision to make. But I would also ask if it is their choice or their child's choice and where they really would like to see their child living.

You know, I cannot say what is right for everyone. I can only really address what's right for our family and I am taking my lead from Demi because Demi is cognitively typical and has made these choices and I am going to try as her parent to make that happen. However, I do understand that there are institutions and that sometimes families have no other option and that may be what they feel is best—what is right for their particular dependent. However, it's not best for our family so I cannot address that. Overall, I work as an advocate to close institutions and have been very much an advocate. People even consider that group homes may not be the correct setting. And I try to encourage all families to see where their child is going to be in the least restrictive environment and in the most community-like setting. And that's why I work with parents, to try to have them envision for their child where their child's going to grow and flourish, be productive to our society, possibly pay taxes and pay for themselves whether they are cognitively involved or not.

I find it most unfortunate that over 50 years ago the first person in the state of California in an iron lung won a lawsuit so he could go to Berkeley University in his iron lung. And I am still fighting for Demi to go to college without any ties legally to her that she should have her own free will. There are three states left in the union at this point that still compromises their medically dependent people. And I am sorry that the state of Alabama is still one of them.

Chapter Eight

JUDITH LYTLE
WARRENVILLE, IL

He went to court to file an injunction to file a temporary restraining order against the state of Illinois in order to secure Jess' nursing services. That was granted on Dec. 13th so she will not lose her nursing services at the age of 21.

Jessica is our biological granddaughter and she will be 21 on Jan. 10th. She was had a typically normal delivery but at nine months became a victim of the shaken baby syndrome. That caused traumatic cerebral palsy and DCFS intervened and she returned home to live with us since she's nine months old. Parental rights were terminated and we adopted her so we are biologically her grandmother, legally her mother and since she turned 18 I'm her co-guardian.

Nine years ago when Jessica had aspiration pneumonia which became necessary to give her a tracheotomy as well as the G-Tube. She was then labeled medically fragile. So when she returned home after thirty-six days in intensive care her primary physician ordered 16 hours a day of nursing care and those are the services she receives until she turns 21. You know when Jessica was adopted she had a DCFS adoption subsidy so we were informed that all of that is terminated when she turns 21.

When a disabled person turns 21 in the state of Illinois two options are given to the family. One to keep the child at home and do all medical care 24-7 themselves or place their child in a nursing home. In Jessica's case because she's trach-ed and g-tubed a nursing home cannot give her the skilled services that she needs she'd actually have to be placed in an intensive care unit of a hospital. For our family that is not an option. Not sure how we were going to handle 24-7 at our ages or lack of expertise but that is the conscientious decision that the family made.

The law would have to be changed and the state of Illinois would have to be mandated to uphold the American's with disabilities Act. And within all the layers of the American's with Disabilities Act there's something called the Olmstead. And Olmstead provides that any disabled person has the right to live where their needs are best met.

I work at Easter Seals Dupage. We have a parent liaison there on staff and they know of all the resources and it was through other parents and the parent liaison at Easter Seals that we learned about attorney Bob Farley.

After Mr. Farley's name was given to us I went on Mr. Farley's website just to get a sense of feel about his mission and his personality. And I got a good feeling.

My daughter and I contacted him to intercede on Jessica's behalf. He went to court to file an injunction to file a temporary restraining order against the state of Illinois in order to secure Jess' nursing services. That was granted on Dec. 13th so she will not lose her nursing services at the age of 21. However, that temporary restraining order is good until the class action suit is settled and of course that could take years. She is part of the class action suit she is the ninth plaintiff.

All of our conversations have been by the phone or via email. But he's been very professional, very quick to answer. I certainly would not hesitate to recommend him to another family.

Ideally, I think all persons with disabilities should have the right to live where they belong and whatever needs need to be met are met. You know we are not asking for 24 hour nursing here in our home we are asking for 16 hours. We are asking for Jessica to have the same right of any other age appropriate kid. Go to school,; get a job do what she can. You know she has a mission there is a reason. I would like Jessica to have the same rights and opportunities as her typical development peers. Whether she uses them or not she should still have them available to her.

The only option presented by Medicaid was that she could be put into a nursing home not with the skill base that she requires because she has a trac, but that she could be at a nursing home and they would pay for that. But to keep her at home they would not offer any financial assistance.

A nursing home? No. That was never a consideration for our family. What I investigated was every other possible resource. There's many programs like TBI which is Traumatic Brain Injury. Because she's a victim of shaken baby she would qualify for the program, however, the program is designed for like a personal attendant for occupational reasons and she doesn't fit that profile. She needs to have an LPN or and RN with her at all times. The family is trained for you know a six to eight hour period but we can't do the same thing that nurses have gone to school for, for years.

She's not spoiled. She pampered and indulged but she's not spoiled. I feel that my husband and I have an exceedingly strong support system starting with our family; all of our kids are involved. We have four biological children all adults. They are all involved at some level. My son does a lot of Jessica's shopping, supply shopping for me. My daughter who lives across the street is amazing she's very hands on gives me a lot of respite. My next daughter lives in New Orleans and when she's here she's very hands-on and our youngest daughter helps to the capacity she can. Two of our daughters are married and both of their husbands are very supportive. We also have an extensive amount of friends as well support from Easter Seals. So I feel embraced by all you know that touch Jessica's life as well as all the lives that Jessica has touched. Jessica is nonverbal as well as non-ambulatory. And because she's non-verbal and because if that trach were to come out she could only live as long as someone could hold their breath so someone is with her. If for some reason the overnight nurse cancels then one of us stays up wide awake in this room all night just in case. Because should she pull out her trach or should she vomit and aspirate we'd have no way of knowing. So she's never ever unattended. When she goes to school her aide is an RN and she rides the bus with her to school, rides the bus back with her. Both my husband and I are retired and though he battles many physical disabilities himself he certainly participates in her life.

Well first of all being alert and awake those 16 hours in addition to the 8 would be like taking care of Jess 24 hours that's virtually impossible for anyone even if I were extremely younger it just can't be done. Also I didn't go to school to learn how to listen to her lungs and she has significant respiratory issues from the battering so we definitely need medical assistance as well as hands on assistance. You need to go to the grocery story you need to take a shower need to do some of those basic everyday things. Do we go on vacation? No, we don't. We definitely take Linda ah, my daughter Linda and I take Jess out as frequently as possible. You know she goes to the beauty shop she goes out to lunch out to the movies she loves going to the theater. We try to do everything age appropriate with her as we would with any of her other peers.

Placing Jessica in a nursing home is not a consideration. Nothing against nursing homes sort of looking forward to the day when I can pick out mine but a regular nursing home doesn't have the staff and manpower to take care of someone like Jess who again someone has to be with her in the room 24/7. It just can't happen she'd have to be in a place that is more like an intensive care unit of a hospital and that would cost just an enormous amount of money so it's just not a consideration. I think she'd shut down. She hasn't had to be hospitalized for four years because we've had at home nursing. That really saves a lot of money and it really says a lot for the positiveness of having home health care. The fact that she hasn't been admitted is just amazing, amazing and enjoyable to us but on the times she has been admitted she shuts down and I'm confident that that would happen if we put her in a nursing home.

Well, they don't have young people in nursing homes. And she doesn't have the ability to play bingo and do some of the other things that some of the other nursing home residents would be and I think she not only has survived here at home in the past nine years when she's worn this label of medically fragile she has thrived and this is where she's happy this is where she's thrived. She doesn't do that when we go to the hospital. We've taken her to a nursing home not for the purpose of placing her but because we have friends and relatives we've wanted to visit. It's just not a place for her. She's 21 she doesn't deserve to be in a nursing home.

Well I think our family subscribes to palliative care and that is quality over quantity and that's pretty much our driving force as we care for Jess.

You know, it's funny that you say that because many people have said, "When are you going to sign the DNR?" Which we prefer to call AND, which is Allow Natural Death and I said the day her bed room turns into her hospital room I'll sign it but until then we are going after quality and we do thoroughly enjoy her and she rocks she absolutely rocks. She brings a lot of joy to all of us.

Well, you know in school someone learned about High School Musical which was the first of the movies that Zach Effron made several years ago and they liked the music in it and so they made a CD of the music and she thoroughly enjoyed it and then when the movie came out we bought it for her and she was one happy girl she was mesmerized. Two years later they did High School Musical 2 another two years they did High School Musical 3. Since then he's really developed as an actor and he has now done 17 Again and Charlie St. Cloud just makes her so happy.

Well she smiles and just lights up when he's on the screen. And if you're sitting and watching her heart rate elevates when he's on the screen alone. When Vanessa's on the screen with him she turns her head and closes her eyes.

And the other interesting thing is there is no way to scientifically test Jess' developmental abilities. There's no way to test her because of her being nonverbal and doesn't have fine motor skills. I know she's at least at the early high school level because of the way she reacts at these movies.

Chapter Nine

KRIS MARKUM

PEMBROKE PINES, FL

I'm constantly guilt ridden, constantly. If we're having
fun and he's not with us I feel guilty.

Well, there is no other like a mother's love. Your intuitions and I can look in my son's eyes and know if he's feeling pain, if he's happy, if he's sad, if he's worried. Nobody else can certainly see that. From a medical standpoint, when doctors look at Conan and they see physically that he needs nursing and he needs all the things that he needs, I see what he goes through and what he's been through, and I know that...what it is that he's feeling. I know that he requires a ventilator 24 hours a day that he requires that machine for every breath that he takes. They're not looking at his feelings; they're looking at him medically.

Conan depends on somebody for everything; for everything; to move his arm, to move his leg, to suction, to scratch him, if he has an itch. Everything. He has to depend on somebody because of his muscle disease, but his brain is perfectly normal. Conan is a very intelligent child. He enjoys movies, puzzles, reading. He is very opinionated. He's very strong willed, and he is very determined in things that he desires.

Growing up, your mom was always there; dad mom, you know someone was always there. Being in the facility, you wait for a visit; you wait...what happens with that...this is his home; this is where he lives. Conan has struggled since his first breath of life. Who is anybody, anybody, to make a decision and take away something from him? Who has the power to force a child to live somewhere away from their family; away from everything they've ever known? Why should a child have to go through that? He already has enough disadvantages in life. Why should he have to be uprooted and put somewhere, and given fear and anxiety and stress? All I can picture is him being in a facility and needing something, or wanting something, and because it's not his turn to go in the room, then he has sit there and wait for that.

Anybody that's ever stayed in a hospital, even one night, they can't wait to go home. You go to work; you can't wait to get home. There's something about going home, I mean like Dorothy, "there's no place like home". So this is his home, so who is anybody to say that he shouldn't stay home, or that he can't stay home?

I prefer for my son to stay at home because he's not homeless. He has a home with his family; his brothers and sisters that lives with him in his home. He has his own room, and it's his own identity and he has all of his things in his own room. He can make choices and decisions for his room, for the things that he wants to do; wants, needs. Going to a facility would cause him to mentally, spiritually die, because he would feel abandoned and I couldn't rest my head at night putting him in a facility. I wouldn't want to be in a facility. I would want to be with my own...with my family, every day.

Conan is in the seventh grade at Hospital Homebound School. A teacher comes to our home and works with him. He also has nursing through Home Health, which they come and help me with him; with his daily activities and needs. He has a respiratory therapist, occupational therapist, physical therapist, speech therapist...

He has a very structured schedule. We try to keep it as structured as possible. The nursing in shifts. A nurse comes early in the morning, generally starts at seven. He requires treatments in the morning, bathing, getting dressed for the day. He has a wheelchair which he sits in intermittent—throughout the day. The therapist comes, and the teachers come, and he's back and forth between the chair and the bed, and then treatments. He requires suctioning. He requires repositioning. He needs to be rotated, changed every two hours. He's on a continuous feeding.

P-Peck is a facility for children. It's a day care for children with disabilities, but the push for him to go there was that they were worried about his socialization, but he doesn't have a problem socializing. That was what I was being told as the reason, but I do know it is because of budget cuts and they were trying to find a reason as to why he needed to be in P-Peck.

They were telling me that, "Oh, he's stuck in his room all day, and there are concern," and I said, "Well, if you send him to P-Peck or put him in a facility he's gonna be in a room all day [Laughter] and so how is that making a difference in the situation?" When I was advised on when he would be picked up to go to the facility, I was told there would be one nurse to every six children that was in transporting.

And I asked, "If my son was having an emergency, how was another child gonna be taken care of it they're having an emergency?" Not to mention if a child is having an emergency, naturally other children is gonna go into a panic knowing there is an emergency happening.

My other concern is some other children don't have their mental capacities, and some of them don't know what's going on in the facility, but my son, he has a muscle disorder, not a brain disorder, so...and a lot of times he gets categorized with being a vegetable and he's not.

The children's needs are not being personalized on an individual basis. They are sent to a facility and it's kind of when an alarm goes off that's when they get attention. When a visitor is coming or they know when a visitor is coming, that's when they get attention, not naturally given attention.

Actually, when I was working, at that time I did not have 24 hour care at that time. My schedule would consist of 4:30 in the morning, getting up and the nurse would leave at five in the morning and I would not have another nurse until like seven in the morning. So from five in the morning until seven in the morning I did not have a nurse, and then at that point, while we were waiting for a nurse, getting ready for work and school, I would go to work and then come home, but as time has gone on, they...the state of Florida, CMS has been cutting back my son's hours.

They were telling me that he was stable, and that he didn't need the hours. When in fact, I have several doctor's notes and visits, and hospital visits stating that he is not stable and he does require 24 hour nursing. When they cut back my hours they wanted him to go to this facility; the P-Peck facility. I said look, the common cold could kill him. Any germ can affect him. He doesn't have the immunity to fight it, and when you're stressed your immunity goes down. He's gonna be stressed. He's gonna be upset. He's not gonna get the proper attention. He is not going to get the proper care that he needs and he will spiritually and mentally shut down if he's sent to this facility.

So the first step that I took was that I appealed the decision that they had made. They had a meeting. I'm not allowed to attend any of these meetings. There is an advocate for you at CMS that is to speak on your behalf, but I'm not allowed to attend the meetings, but they're making a decision on my life and my son's life; and my livelihood and my son's livelihood, but we're not allowed to attend the meeting.

They said that my appeal was denied and that he still needs to go to the facility. I still had not known at that point that it was a social issue that they said they were concerned about. After my appeal they said, "Because socially they're worried about him." So then, I was like, "That's never been an issue before. He socializes. He has cousins, brother and sisters, family members and neighbors come in and he socializes." So then I got letters come in that says, his therapist filled out a social test and he was fine, just to show them that he doesn't have any social issues.

I could not go to sleep at night knowing that I was putting my child in an abusive situation; what I felt as an abusive situation. Because his needs would not be met physically, mentally, you know, his needs would not be met to the best that he could have. I'm not gonna put him in a situation where I know he's going to get ill, and he could die. I couldn't put him in that situation.

So when I appealed it, they told me, "No", "absolutely not! He has to go to the facility." So I said, "Well, I'm not sending him there." So they said, "We're not sending a nurse during the hours he's supposed to go to the facility."

First I used paid-time off to stay with him and then from paid-time off, I did FMLA, the Family Leave of Absence. And from the Family

Leave of Absence that is also...you only have ninety days for that as well. Basically my work said to me, "We understand what you're going through, but we need somebody here full-time." Everything was in appeals which takes months and weeks. I ran out of paid time off.

But eventually, every two or three months whenever they decide to have a meeting, they have a meeting to decide if you have to have nursing care or if you have to go to the facility. So we're in the dark on a constant rollercoaster of emotions.

As much as you try to keep your life structured and stable, you feel like at any moment you know what's gonna happen. You never know what is going to be said; what they're gonna take from you; what you can have; what you can't have.

Although, over time, his health has declined and more has been taken away, and I ask them to explain to me how his health is declining, but he's getting less. That doesn't make any sense to me. So my only thought on that is that they're not wanting to spend the money or money's being spent elsewhere, I don't know.

The most difficult thing, and even with any mother without any child with a disability, is finding balance, and structure, and I try my best to balance everything. There are times when my other children feel, I'm sure, "Oh mommy I miss you," you know, if I'm at the hospital for a week, and they're with their grandmother. Doctor's appointments and I'm very mentally wiped. Hard days I may not feel like staying up watching a moving with them 'cause I'm just too exhausted, but you know I try to balance as best that I can. They understand; they're also two very bright compassionate children.

They understand! They understand! But of course they feel at time, and there are times when I know Conan feels the same way, so it's a...I'm constantly guilt ridden, constantly.

If we're having fun and he's not with us I feel guilty. If we're in the pool, he can't go. But we try to do things to have balance and structure and to give him the best and happiest life and best opportunities.

That's what I want for him, is to have the very best advantages and opportunities that he can, because he was already handed a very big disadvantage in life and I don't think it's fair or right for anybody to make a decision to take his home and his family away from him, and to put him in a dangerous situation, because that's abusive.

Chapter Ten

SHEILA DRUCKER
NORFOLK, VA

What we found was absolutely shocking. When we went up to the ward, which was essentially a relatively small area that housed 27 children, just 27 children; it was half of a floor and that was it.

Virginia has a system of lawyers called Guardian Ad Litems. Most States have attorneys that represent children and are appointed to represent children who are abused and neglected. In Virginia, they're called Guardian Ad Litems and we have to go through certain certifications on a yearly basis to maintain that ability to represent children who cannot speak for themselves.

My job as a Guardian Ad Litem is to conduct an investigation. My job is to be independent of the courts, of social services, of the guardians, of the parents, or any other institutions that might be involved in the child's life.

I was appointed the Guardian Ad Litem for Qualeigh's one-year old sister, and she presented with two types of fractures which cannot be sustained in an accidental manner; they were intentional injuries that she presented with at a local Children's Hospital.

Because of that, his siblings were basically deemed to being at risk for neglect, and he was actually found to being neglected. The siblings of Qualeigh were essentially removed from the guardian who is the biological mother; they were removed. We found out that she had a history of parental neglect, and especially medical neglect. She did not handle her son's case; the one who had this Brachial Plexus Injury at birth – that's otherwise called Erb's Palsy. She did not handle that in a responsible fashion and that child had lost a precious window of opportunity to have a successful repair, as well as a life where he was not disabled by the non-use of his right arm.

We determined that the mother did not even do "well baby checks" for her children. They weren't getting vaccinated at the right time, and that she has a history of instability in terms of where she lived and although she didn't have apparent mental health difficulties, she was psychologically evaluated. It was very clear she had what we call a personality disorder, and that's basically what the psychologist who evaluated her found.

She was given a year period of time in order to remedy the conditions; in order for her to be re-awarded custody of her children. Well, that really never happened and she never was, but there was a family member who assumed custody.

Qualeigh was not part of the case. Nobody knew anything about Qualeigh. Nobody knew that he even existed. He was basically invisible at the time we were in court. In the course of my investigation, I learned that there was another child; Qualeigh, her first born, who was at an institution locally, which is essentially known as an adult nursing home, not a place where children are normally placed called Lake Taylor Hospital.

That hospital has a reputation of being an elderly nursing facility or a rehab facility for adults who have had serious injuries, that are elderly that need additional assistance in terms of being rehabilitated. Frankly, even though I am born and raised in Norfolk Virginia and I've been in practice for more than 24 years, at that point in time back in May 2008, I didn't even know that Lake Taylor Hospital had a ward where children lived.

I brought this to the court's attention and together with a social worker who was assigned to the case; a very good social worker, her name is Cheryl Perry and she still is very active in Norfolk and now she works for a private agency.

We got permission from the court to go visit this child, Qualeigh, over at the hospital and really what we were expecting to find was a child who was really incapable of leading -- what one would consider to be -- a normal existence, in other words, in a home. We were expecting to find a child so incapacitated that the institutionalization from the time of birth would make sense.

What we found was absolutely shocking.

I remember the very moment in time that we both saw him and we came up to the ward. We didn't give them any advance notice. We came in basically with an order from the court, and we let them know that she was a social worker from Norfolk Social Services, and I was an attorney that was asked by the court to go an meet the sibling of my client; because Qualeigh was not my client at that point and time, and there are rules of privacy that supersede my ability to go visit a child at an institution – and the hospital was cooperative.

When we went up to the ward, which was essentially a relatively small area that housed 27 children, just 27 children; it was half of a floor and that was it.

I was greeted by a child that was basically doing wheelies in a wheelchair up and down the hallway, and was communicating basically with some type of electronic device, and he also knew sign language. I started talking to the charge nurse, and I asked her some questions, and it was just very clear to me that this was a child that had Cerebral palsy; that was basically born with brain damage that effected motor functioning, but it was also very clear to me that cognitively, he understood everything that was going on; he was able to communicate; he clearly had the ability of maneuvering, and he was a joyful child. He was joyful! When I looked around the ward that he was in, I saw children who were basically lying in cribs; who were incapacitated, definitely physically unclear to the extent that they were cognitively disabled.

It appeared that all these 27 children were in one physical area; half of the floor of the wing, essentially, on this one floor.

It appeared to be all open space, and there was a lot of nursing. It wasn't as medically sophisticated as a neo-natal intensive-care unit, but there were clearly monitors that monitored children's saturation rates; there were clearly a lot of children there. There were gastronomy tube fed; there were some babies; a couple of older kids. I wasn't able to see all of them, but I didn't see any of the other children with the kind of mobility Qualeigh had; or the interaction.

The nursing and social work staff at the hospital described Qualeigh as "The smartest child there," and one of my main reasons for being there – frankly my only reason for going there — was to conduct an investigation on the mother's ability to care for the other sibling, and what better way is to see, well what has she done for her own child that's been in the institution.

Again, we were shocked to find out that, not only did Qualeigh not know his mother, but that most of the staff at this hospital – other than the social work staff - didn't know the mother as well. It was reported that she only came to visit him basically once a year on Christmas.

So, I asked the question, I said, "Well, you know...does this child have any family? Does anyone come to see him? How long has he been here? What does he do?" And again, I found out that he had been basically living in this ward for close to six years. And I don't believe, I don't think he ever went outside.

The day I visited coincidentally, he had this new wheelchair and he was very proud of it. They apparently had a lot of hassle in terms of getting funding because it was a very sophisticated electronic wheelchair for him that gave him a lot of mobility.

His mother met us up there that day, and again, she did not know how to communicate with him. I asked her, "Well, don't you know sign language?" And she said "No." I said "Why Not?" And she said, "Well, she's "learning," which turned out to be not true.

I made further inquiries after that day. I was so affected by the fact that this child who, frankly, did not appear any different to me than children that we see on a daily basis out in society in malls, in restaurants, in movie theaters, bowling allies and in schools, who basically have Cerebral palsy and are being wheeled by various people and they're participating in everything that we participate in, with the exception of certain motor skills, I didn't understand why he was there, number one.

In a place where there were hardly any children that wasn't child friendly, we also have a hospital locally called St. Mary's Infant Home for Children, where children do live for long periods of time, but it's reputed to be a good institution and it is kid-friendly; it's only for children. They just built a brand new facility locally; it was very nice; it was very clean. I've been there many times. I have other clients there. None of those questions were readily answered for me.

The social work staff at the hospital was not cooperative. They didn't want anyone intruding in or asking a lot of questions. There was a young social worker who was responsible for Qualeigh's case; who had been very frustrated with his mother for the past two years and had gone out of her way to provide transportation for the mother to see Qualeigh, but it still didn't happen; to try and be the impetus for a strong relationship between the two, or some relationship, that didn't work.

His medical records which I later gained access to after being appointed as his lawyer; his medical record shows tremendous frustration on the part of the doctors who came to visit him and to treat him; a lot of specialists in the area did not feel that the child should have been there. They thought that child should be in this other institution; St. Mary's Infant Home, which still begs the question as to "Why you should be institutionalized in the first place?" But the medical records indicated why is this child not—at least—at St. Mary's. According to the social work staff, they had tried to get the mother to complete the application package with their help, to St. Mary's, but she simply preferred having Qualeigh there because she was more comfortable with him being there.

This was a child that was neglected in every sense of the word because every child deserves a parent. Without that parent; without that family they're not going to develop properly. They're not gonna have any attachment bonding, which is a very critical phase in a child's life which creates a whole host of problems later on if you don't have that attachment.

There was no Guardian Ad Litem for this child because our state has no procedure by which an institutionalized child immediately gets a Guardian Ad Litem, and in this case, this child's situation should have been reported to our local Child Protective Services, but again, because he's institutionalized, they would have refused to have filed any type of protective orders, or done anything on behalf of that child.

Qualeigh got there in the first place, because he was born with brain damage, and because his mother was either unwilling or unable to take care of him. She never relinquished physical or legal custody. His mother was still the custodian; the legal custodian. Her name; her signature had to be on every single paper work for every single surgical procedure and medical procedure that he had, but it was only in name, there was no summons substance to that relationship.

He had a tracheotomy and he was on a ventilator when he was born. That hospital has a specialization in children who—it's called vent therapy; ventilator therapy.

Qualeigh's continued institutionalization from essentially the time of birth, and the fact that he had a parent who was not just not involved, but one who he really did not know in any meaningful fashion, highlights the fact that there was no parent education. His mother thought, because he has a gastronomy tube: in other words he was fed through G-tube directly into his stomach, because he did not have the ability because of neurological and motor issues to eat by mouth, she thought that that's what required his institutionalization. Whereas, when I met him, he was essentially feeding himself; he was holding the tube, and pouring the formula, and letting it drip by gravity, into his stomach. People can live their entire lives with gastronomy tubes.

I'm not saying he should not have been hospitalized for a period of time when he was extremely young, maybe from one to three, when he was still ventilator dependent, but once he was off that ventilator, in other words, once he could breathe on his own and once his tracheotomy was removed—which it was for close to over a year by the time I met him—there was no reason to continue to institutionalize him, or at least for 24-hour medical care, which is what was going on there.

The hospital took no steps to give him a better life. They're existing essentially on Medicaid dollars. My understanding is that there was a waiting list to get into that hospital for some reason, than into St. Mary's, so I don't understand why somebody would have petition the court in some fashion to say, "This is a child that's in need of services, and in need of protection; let's do something about it! But nobody did that, because from a legal point of view, he had a mother who was still his legal custodian.

I left there in tears that day, and it takes a lot; I've practiced for a long time, and have seen a lot of things that are very heartbreaking...very heartbreaking! This was one of the worst things I had ever seen. It was basically, basically, animals had a better life than this child had. Then the lack of stimulation...of course, he was in a school there, they had a special school, which Virginia and most states are required to have. In other words, every child is entitled to an education, so they have a special education school there, which brings me to Michelle Martin.

So I was asking some questions, "Who does this child have a relationship with?" and one of the staff basically contacted me later on; I left my card there, and as if this was an undercover operation; as if they were putting their jobs in jeopardy they said to me, "Please don't tell anyone that we're calling you, but there is an employee that used to work here at the hospital who absolutely loves this child, in fact, she even comes in to do his laundry."

I said, "Why does she have to do his laundry, don't you do the laundry?"

And they said, "Well you know, a lot of the children's items, when they get washed in the hospital, they get lost."

And I'm thinking to myself well "Well, "if somebody's coming to do somebody's laundry, they really must love that person, especially when they don't have to."

So I was able to find Ms. Martins, through my own means, and I contacted her, and she basically told me that she had been a teacher's aide at this special education school there at the hospital, and really formed a very strong bond with Qualeigh and she was doing a lot of things for him in her capacity as a teacher's aide, but also during off-hours, and that the hospital administration frowned upon that and basically told her that that had to end, because she was basically playing

60

favorites within the scope and course of her duties as a teacher's aide. So she resigned her position.

She's a very religious woman, religious in the sense of the word that gives good meaning to the word...a real Christian lady. I'm Jewish, and I don't find many people who utilize those terms correctly, but she was the walking epitome of someone who has a pure heart and put her money where her mouth was. She meant every word. She said she had been praying on this for over a month and she knew that when she walked out of that hospital that she was going to have custody somehow, but she didn't know how to do it, because she never talked to the mother.

We were able to set up a meeting between Qualeigh's mother and Ms. Martins, and even though she initially was resistant to the idea of relinquishing custody, I basically made it very clear to her, that once Ms. Martins filed a custody petition with my assistance, and once I was appointed as Qualeigh's Guardian Ad Litem, that I would be—in no uncertain terms—recommending that Ms. Martins be awarded full custody. So that she could either cooperate or not cooperate, it was up to her.

In the end she ended up cooperating.

Although she wanted to retain, when we finally went to court and after Ms. Martins did file her custody petition, the mother was still in basically in an unrealistic world of "I still want to be this child's mother" for some reason, the judge wouldn't even hear about it when he learned of Qualeigh's story.

The mother was given curtain visitation rights, with reasonable notice to Ms. Martins, but it is my understanding that she's only exercised them once a year.

Qualeigh has been with Ms. Martins, I believe, close to two years now. Ms. Martins is a very unusual person. She's a very nurturing woman. She's a very spiritual woman, and she's a very loving woman. She has two children that are doing very well. She's raised other relatives in her extended family. She has a very supportive husband. These are not wealthy people. These are people who believe that they receive pleasure and happiness out of giving to others, and they expect very little in return.

Her husband seems as good as gold; they have a wonderful partnership. They have a vibrant and joyful home life, and Qualeigh is a part of that; he is a son to them. I mean, she couldn't have done this if her husband had not supported her.

Again, at the time that I met this young child, I've been in practice 23 years, I am now 52 years of age, and you can add three years on to that, and I can count people that I have met in my life like Ms. Martin on one hand.

I was in the right place at the right time. I'm not important in this story. I simply saw a problem and I could have either walked away from it because that wasn't my legal obligation at that point and time, or I could have done something about it. As we get older, sometimes we decide it's just time to do something about it, and in the process I learned a lot about the manner in which we as a society are basically turning away from children and adults who are institutionalized.

I've met many people now in this line of work who have basically said, "There is no reason to institutionalize any child." And it's my understanding that when I first got involved in this case there was a new program called Money Follows the Person where Virginia had billions of dollars at its disposal to essentially start a de-institutionalization, and placing these children in community-based settings; whether they are homes, or group homes, whatever model they wanted to use, but that never took place, and to this day and now we're at 2011 and we're basically one month into a Department of Justice study of Virginia, that says, "Virginia, you've got to get your act together;" – "you're one of the few states that hasn't even closed down one state-run institution." It takes less money to put children in individual homes, but it just take a lot of effort to figure it out and we're light-years away from it. That's what I learned.

The Department of Justice is breathing on Virginia's neck and forcing Virginia to do what it should have done in the very beginning. There still is an issue, legally.

This highlights an issue. Why do we institutionalize? And this child's case just highlights; he's only one child, out of probably thousands.

Well, think of it this way. If you or I had been born in a hospital and we had no parents, and we were essentially being raised by the hospital staff who are very nice to us, but of course we know the hospital staff changes; people come and go, what would we be like if we weren't able to play outside, or go to the movies, or go out in the world and see other people, or touch and pet an animal, or have interactions with other children on a continual basis that we could intelligently relate to, what would our lives be like?

This child has a home, now. He has a family. He has a father. He has a mother. He has a dog. He has siblings. He has his own room. He has activities. He plays in T-ball. I mean, this child plays on T-ball. He didn't know anything about T-ball before then. He has a full life. He has potential...whatever that potential is. He has love. He never had that kind of stability before.

I mean, if I had not been appointed as the Guardian Ad Litem for his sibling; if the mother had not created this situation where the sibling had sustained these physical injuries, he'd still be at Taylor Hospital. It's as simple as that!

I don't know what he would have done. He would have just continued to live his life in that small little, half of a floor, in that one hospital.

Chapter Eleven

MICHELLE MARTINS
NORFOLK, VA

When God gives me something, especially something I don't think I can handle I do it to the best of my abilities, and that was like with Qualeigh. I knew that it was for me to have Qualeigh, 'cause God has a mission for him. God has a purpose for him. There is something that God wants Qualeigh to do, and I'm a tool to help him accomplish what God wants him to do.

I married my husband Jose Martins, in 1990, and we adopted two boys, Alex and Michal, and then when they became teenagers, we had Jahkeem, who is 13 now, and then four years later then we had Joseph and Joshua, he was a twin and then one of them passed away.

Well, I had retired out of the Navy in 2003, and moved around for about a year. Then started going to school at TCC to be Early Childhood Education field. Jahkeem, my 13 year old, he's autistic, so he was in a program called CSAP, and he had his tri-annual. So we went up to get his testing done to qualify for him to stay in the program. Well he blew his test away, and the lady asked me was I working, and I told her not at that time, and I was going to school, and she ask me what was I doing, and I told her I was going to school for Education.

So she asked me if I wanted a job, and I said, "Ok!" So she gave me an application, and so I told her I'll bring it back, but she insisted that I fill it out right then and there. So I had filled out the application, and that was a Tuesday, and that Wednesday they called me in and I started working for CSAP. I was at St. Mary's home for disabled children. Then a month or two after that, I got transferred, and that was November 2006, and that's when I met Qualeigh, and so it was love at first sight!

It was November 6, 2006. I know the date! And it was different 'cause it was at a hospital and they took me up and showed me the kids that would be in our classroom. They introduced Qualeigh last, 'cause he was in his bed, which is an enclosed bed, it zip closed. The nurse said, "You don't wanna touch him, he's real messy, he's real messy." And when I looked at him and stuff, he had mucus all over his face, and he was a mess basically, but there was just something about him that I just fell in love with him.

Lake Taylor Transitional Care Hospital is the name of the place, and the Children's ward is 2West. There are six kids to each cubicle, and the cubicles are about this size of the living room right here, so I would say about an 18 by 20 room. There was only windows at the end of the cubicle which was Qualeigh's side, and it was very compact, 'cause of the size of the cribs, with all their equipment and their clothes and everything. It wasn't a whole lot of room. Then you have the children who were in wheelchairs, so it's not a lot of room. They had two TVs. There's one TV per cubicle, so they would have the TV toward the nursing station, the hallway part, to face the nurses so they could watch TV.

Some of the children are on ventilators and some are not. Qualeigh was one of the children that were not on a ventilator. Some of the children that were on ventilators were not as mobile. They were on regular hospital beds. Children like Qualeigh and one of the other kids. It was two enclosed cribs at the end of his cubicle that he was in, and it was him and another boy. To me, I would call it a cage. It's an oversized crib with a plastic dome on the top. That's where he was kept most of the time, if he was not in school; he was in bed most of the time.

And he had a real bad habit of digging in his throat, 'cause he has real bad lung disease, so he has a lot of thick secretions, but he cannot cough it up, so the only way to get it out is if he digs it up. So a lot of time he would dig in his mouth and pull it up and stuff, and just wipe it wherever, because he had no other teaching, because no one ever taught him what to do with the stuff.

He drools really bad, and he loves to grab things. My opinion was the reason why he grabs things was for attention. I think children do things just to get attention. If you get a response out of people, then you will continue to do it, that's my opinion, but the nurses didn't care for that too much.

They would leave him in that crib with no TV on, no radio on...nothing...nobody interacting with him. And he had adapted to it and he would just sit there...in his crib just like this, all the time.

So he was just busy. He was always grabbing on stuff; he was always pulling on stuff. And when he was in his wheelchair and you took your eye off of him, he was gonna move, 'cause he would bounce his wheelchair and get around. He was in a lot. It was something about him that was different. I fell in love with him

Their clothes are all washed together. A lot of the kids' clothes got mixed up together. It was just crowded; it's very crowded up there. They don't get any personal care, cause it's like a routine, everything is a routine, everything is on a schedule. The Certified Nursing Assistants, they clean the children on a rotation, not as needed, but on a time schedule. And most of the children up there, they're not potty trained or anything, so they don't know a routine, they don't know a routine to go on, so when they have the urge to go, they just go 'cause they have diapers on. So a lot of time, like for Qualeigh, he didn't like it on him, so if they had already went through and just changed him and he went, he's gonna take his diaper off and just paint with it basically. He wasn't really painting, he had it on him and he was trying to get it off. And if he had something on his hands and stuff, he's gonna wipe it, 'cause he don't like things on his hands, so he will wipe it wherever he could. And so it will be a mess, but I would think that if a child has a mess on him just change him, and you know with us working with them, a lot of time we would tell the CN 'such and such just used the bathroom', 'cause we were not allowed to change them. We were there just to educate them at a point, and we spent time with them to keep them busy.

I worked from September to June, and then I worked from June to July for the summer for the regular school rotation.

In the first year, I was getting to know everything and by the second year, I had grown really close to Qualeigh, and so that's when I introduced my family to Qualeigh. So we would start spending after work time with him and we would go up there on the weekends. My husband and the children we would go up there and just sit with him and talk with him.

Then I asked if we could take the kids off the floor, because some of the kids at Lake Taylor went to different classrooms; they had two different classrooms, they had one on the second floor; they had one on the first floor—and those were the older kids, the teenagers. They went to classrooms.

So I asked, can we take them off the ward? And she was like, 'let me get the respiratory.' So the first time we tried to wheel Qualeigh pass the doors, he grabbed the doors, and I mean he was just crying. He pulled his bib over his face, and was like, 'No! NO!' He kept signing, 'I don't wanna go, I don't wanna go!' He was scared! And so when I took him back they checked his heart-rate and his heart-rate was like 176. He was just terrified, and so we had to slowly work towards that. Then the teacher was like, 'well, everyday, we'll just let him sit by the door.' So for the first couple of weeks we would just let him sit by the door and watch people get on and off the elevator, and walk pass. So he finally started inching away from the door, going pass the door, which was cool.

Then he would let us take him just on the same floor, the second floor. We would roll him around. He wouldn't get on the elevator or anything. Then we started working toward the elevator. We would let him push the button on the elevator and a couple weeks after that we finally coaxed him into getting on the elevator. So each step was like a little process to get him beyond that.

So then we finally got him on the first floor, and he would roll around the first floor. Then we finally started working on him to go outside.

He was afraid. He would just cry! He would get all jumpy and he would just cry. He would cover his face with his bib and he would just continue to cry and his heart rate would go up and so we would have to back off.

Mostly every step that we went we would have to sit with him by that next step. We would have to sit by the door, then we would have to sit by the elevator, and we would have to sit by the glass door so he could just look outside, to get him to that next stage. And he would finally work up the courage to go that next stage, but it took a process. We eventually got him to go outside. We'd take him to the playground area that he really enjoyed once he got used to it. They have a swing that you could roll the children on with their wheelchair. So then he would ride the swing and he got to look at the butterflies everything and flowers and stuff, and so he really enjoyed that once he got accustomed to going out there.

And so then once we got him used to going outside, we would take him outside more and so we had built a rapport with him.

The first time that I took him out of Lake Taylor, we went to Disney On Ice, and that was something else getting him in my van. It was like, 'Oh my gosh!' Because he was holding on to the door, and he was just crying.

They had the Disney on Ice out at Hampton VA, so we went there. My husband picked up the boys and I picked up Qualeigh and we all me there. It was at the Hampton Coliseum and it is very hard to get somebody in a wheelchair into that place, cause you have to push them up this ramp and I thought I was gonna die by the time we got up to our seats.

But they all enjoyed themselves. He really enjoyed Disney On Ice and at the end they had the bubbles and everything and so he was all excited. We had a wonderful time. My husband bought him some toys. And so we were going back and I was putting Qualeigh in my van and the boys were gonna go with Jose and everybody breaks out and starts crying.

So now I got three little boys just a crying; just 'boohoo' crying. Qualeigh's crying 'cause he don't wanna leave the other two; JT and Joseph are crying 'cause they don't want Qualeigh to leave, and Joseph

68

was like, 'why do you have to take him back?' And it's like, 'I could only keep him a certain amount of time.' So JT turns around and ask me, 'did you sign him out?' And I was like, 'No you don't just sign him out,' he was like, 'they won't know the difference.' I laughed. I was like, 'I have to take him back. I can't just keep him.' I said, 'y'all gonna make me go to jail.'

So we finally got everybody understanding; we kinda sort of got everybody to stop crying. But by time I got Qualeigh back to Lake Taylor, he was no good. He cried and he cried. When I left there, they said he eventually had to cry himself to sleep, 'cause he didn't wanna go back there.

Then Qualeigh fell out of his crib one day and I had got really upset about that. And I had got a lecture from the Principal telling me that my relationship with Qualeigh was inappropriate and they didn't encourage it. So after that, every time somebody would do something that I didn't like about Qualeigh I was very voicy about it and so, I got reprimanded again about my relationship with Qualeigh. So when it came time for me to sign up for the next school year, I refused. I didn't want to be there anymore, so I left. I didn't go back. I didn't go back anymore except to see Qualeigh. I told them that in a year's time he would be living with me and I wouldn't have to worry about anybody telling me what I can and cannot do with Qualeigh...not knowing that it would come true.

One day in July I was at ODU, getting ready to sign up for school and one of the nurses called me from Lake Taylor, and she told me "There's a lawyer and social worker up here asking questions about Qualeigh and the lawyer wanna meet you." So we talked, and then Sheila Drucker came and met us, and she asked us what do we wanna do, and so my husband and I we was like, "We would like to get him out of there."

But we knew we couldn't afford it because we know how much adoption is, and so she explained to us how to do it where it wouldn't cost us anything. So we were like "Ok!" So she did it Pro-bono, and she eventually became...after we went to social services and we eventually met his birth mom – which was an exciting day—it was his birthmother, his aunt, and a lot of social workers and lawyers. She had her lawyer up there 'cause she had got in some situation with her other three kids.

So we were all in one room and we were talking. They introduced her to me and she had... she wasn't too pleased about it, and so her attitude was "Who are you trying to take my child away from me?"

At first I was angry at her, because I knew for a fact that he was up there for six years, and she never went up there to visit him. She had no contact with him or anything. She never signed any of his IEPs; none of his school papers. She never got a copy of his birth certificate. This is stuff that I knew because dealing with the school.

My husband had already told me 'just keep your cool; keep your cool!' So she vented out. And I explained to her that I wasn't trying to take Qualeigh away from her or anybody. I wasn't trying to replace her. I just loved him and wanted to give him something better than what he had.

They would give him narcotics just to keep him calm, and it just wasn't right. He wasn't expressive; he wasn't learning anything, because he was locked up most of the time. And that produced his behavior. And all I wanted to do was to give him something more than what he had at the time. So and I explained that to her and she kind of understood but she wasn't too happy about it. They explained to her that she really didn't have too much say-so on it because of the fact that they were taking the other children from her. So after they did our background check and seeing that we didn't have any criminal records and our finances were ok they authorized us to go apply for custody.

So I went down to city hall, and I applied for custody, and that was in August 2008 and that was the beginning of our process.

October of 2008, we were granted temporary custody of him, and so I took my paperwork back to Lake Taylor because they were saying I didn't have any right to him and I couldn't go see him anymore, because legally I had no right to go see him. So after that, I took my paper up there and explained to them, this is what I want to do, I want to process him out of there.

So they came up with a plan on how to take care of him medically and they told me I had to do it with his mother, which I didn't understand at the time, so I didn't say anything, because I just wanted to get it done.

And so, for the first month, I would stop and pick her up, which was uncomfortable because we didn't have a relationship. So I'd pick her up and we would go to the hospital and we would start doing our training which she didn't want to do half of it.

So I had got fed up with it, so I called the lawyer, and she was like, 'well, why is she going up there', and I was like, 'cause they told her to'.

So then Sheila Drucker went up there to the hospital explained to them that the biological mother had nothing to do with what I was doing and they was like, 'Oh, OK!' So we found out that I didn't have to have her with me, it was just my husband and I that needed to do the training. So we did all the training, we learned how to change his G-Tube, how we feed him; how to give him his meds; he didn't have the tracheal in—so we went through that process. We had to do it three different times, and so we went through all that, we got qualified.

And they finally gave us a date to bring him home which was December 18, 2008. The boys were really just paranoid about that, 'cause they didn't quite understand what was going on, as in how long he was gonna stay. So that night we all slept in his room and it was nice. They didn't wanna go to school the next day, 'I had to make them go to school. So they went to school for a least a couple of days and then we had winter break. So then we just spent all our time in Qualeigh's room. So then Christmas, I have a brother and sister, who live down the street and so we were going down there, but he was in a wheelchair, and I didn't know how he would do.

So I call myself putting him back in the van to just drive him down there, which I didn't know that I had basically terrorized him. Cause to put him in my van, he went back to the same routine; he wouldn't get in the van, he would hold on to the door, and he would just cry and he would just cry. And I didn't understand what was wrong with him. 'We're just going down the street!' 'We're just going down the street!' So then when we went around the corner and we pulled up down there

71

and was getting him out the van and he gives me this GREAT BIG OLE HUG. So finally it dawned on me, he thought I was taking him back to Lake Taylor. And it was like, 'nooo, I'm not gonna take you back,' 'I'm not gonna leave you.' So he got really scared about that.

And then we finally got him in school. We had to get special permission to get him back in school because he did not have all his immunizations, and he had to have all his immunizations in order for him to go to Norfolk Public School. And we just naturally assumed that...'cause he was in the hospital, he would have all his immunizations, but he didn't.

So we had the doctor, Dr. Moneymaker wrote a letter explaining that they couldn't give him his shots all at one time. So he got his first set of shots in January. Then we had to wait six months later to get his second shots, and then we had to wait another six months later, so now he's up to date with all his immunizations. But he didn't have any of them, and so that made me question, 'does any of the children get their immunizations that live in institutions?' It makes you wonder!

His teeth were bad. And if you ever get to see any children in the institution, look at their teeth—'cause most of the time they don't brush their teeth. They don't take care of them, you know like, like a person who takes care of their own child in their home.

November of 2008 was the first time Qualeigh had seen the dentist, which was different, because they had to sedate him and he had a lot of buildup; plaque buildup and he had a fusion with the bottom of his tongue and his mouth, so his tongue was actually stuck, so they had to cut it lose. Now what we're doing with his teeth is; they removed seven of his baby teeth to get his adult teeth to grow in. So he has five more baby teeth to get pulled out, which will probably be in about six months when we get those pulled out. Then his adult teeth will come in.

Then they'll go and break his jaw and lower it so that he'll be able to close his mouth...because right now, his mouth is closed, but it's open in the front 'cause the back is already touching. So they're gonna lower his jaw so he can have that free movement, so he could close the front of his mouth.

He had a lot of medical issues; he had a lot of medicine when I first got custody of him, so I spend most of my days giving him medicine. Now he's down to iron, multivitamins, his inhaler, Albuterol and the Pulmicort. And then we give him Benefiber, as needed, and that's it. Oh, and his eye-drops. He was legally deaf; could not hear. He hears fine now. He's passed his hearing tests. He hears very well. That wax had turned into rocks in his ears. They had classified him as blind, legally blind. But he's had surgery on his eyes and everything, so as you notice he wears glasses now. So his eyesight is a lot better. He sees very well now.

His legs were a negative 75. They were always bent in this position like a sitting position, and that comes from constantly being in his wheelchair. That was the only way he moved his legs. But now his right leg is a -6 and his left leg is a -8, so now he can basically stretch is legs all the way out. He walks around the house and he does really good moving around with his walker. He can move independently with his walker.

Sometimes you just need to guide him in the direction that he needs to go, but he does very well moving around by his self.

Jahkeem, Joseph, and Qualeigh play T-Ball together. This is their third year of playing together. Qualeigh doesn't ride with me most of the time when we go places, because I teach Sunday school, so I have to be to church earlier than the rest of them. So Jose brings the boys to church. So their together...especially on weekends, 'cause Saturday they got T-Ball or practice or whatever, and Sunday they come to church together, and then I have Sunday School. Then like on the third and fourth Sunday I have to usher, and on the first and second Sunday, I got the nursery 'cause I'm the director of the Church nursery.

I don't like the outside, so they're with him more during the summertime, and the pool time, and like, play time. They play with him more than I do. I don't really play with him; play with him, you know, like the Wii, and game outside and stuff. That's not my forte. They spend more time with him.

He's good with baseball and boxing; the boxing one. He's good with that. A lot of times...you have make sure you put the cord around his hand 'cause if not, he'll drop it. He loves music. He got that from my husband. He loves to listen to music. They will sit in that play room and they just listen to the radio and sing and they'll dance and stuff like that.

He likes Sponge Bob and that's from my sister. My sister kept him one day and they just watch Sponge Bob all day long. So now he loves Sponge Bob. Then they bought him all these cds; Sponge Bob DVDs, so, its play time mostly with them. Then like outside, my husband has a...it's a ball attached to a string, hanging from the tree. That's their practice ball. So they'll be out there and I could watch them from the kitchen window so. But I'll watch them and they all take turns and they bat, hit the ball and stuff. Sometimes somebody gets hit in the head with the ball, but it's a soft ball. But they are out there playing with that, or they ride their bikes, Qualeigh's in his wheelchair, and then they like to push him, going up and down the street and stuff in his wheelchair, which they think is cool.

He's learning to write. And I believe he will be successful. Whatever he chooses to do, he'll be able to accomplish it. And he'll be living on his own. That much I do know! I know that he will be living on his own, and providing for his self. He is a determined little boy.

Everything that comes his way...he problem solves things, and he is determined to learn and do whatever it is. Like when he's afraid of trying new things, but he doesn't give up. Like with his walker, he was scared to death. But now he can hold your fingers and he could walk through this whole house. You can give him his walker and he'll walk through this whole house. He walks a block. He walks a whole block down the street just to go down to my brother's house. Sometimes he gets a little lazy 'cause if he don't see my brother's car out there, he'll want to come home.

I have medical papers from a doctor saying that he would be on a ventilator all his life, but by time he was three he was off the ventilator, so their predictions of him were off key. And I understand that doctors are not suppose to give you that high hope so you won't be let down, so they make things sound worse than they really are, but sometimes you need that to get you to go; to make you work harder for them.

The difference between us here in the house and the institution; institutions are like a factory. Things are just constantly done on routine. You go step by step according to this piece of paper telling you 'this is what you need to do for the day.'

There is no personal touch to it. There's nobody. You tell a CNA this child needs to get cleaned, but you got one CNA for 12 children. So you got one person that's going through changing diapers, washing faces, taking care of these children. As the nurses sit and actually just give out the medicine. The CNA are the ones that actually bath the children, change their clothes, change their diapers, do all their hygiene care. What they're trying to do is speed. You got one person with 12 children just speeding through something.

Here, you got us, with one child. You got a multiple of people with one child. So yes, he gets more personal care. I take my time when I brush his teeth. I don't just take the toothbrush and run through there, so his breath can smell better. And they never really brush their teeth in there. They have these sponge things with mouthwash or something and they rub it around inside their mouth.

They look at children differently in an institution than I or we look at children in a home setting. So he was classified as being there long-term. His mother had no interest in taking care of him and she really didn't sign any paperwork. Qualeigh was classified as to be there for the rest of his life.

When I first got custody of Qualeigh, that next week, we had to go to the emergency room. Come to find out that he had pneumonia, and it was so bad that they hospitalized him. When they took the X-ray his lungs were white masses; it was that much mucus in there. He had pneumonia seven times that first year. We stayed at the hospital. Because every time he have that cough or that smell to him – it's a smell he gets, because he's got lung disease basically, from not caring.

God set up the whole thing! Because, if it were left up to me, that's an area that I would not have gone to. I have my own personal issues. I don't like to mess with anybody's mouth. I think the mouth is the nastiest place to ever venture. So like when my kids started losing their teeth and everything, I would send them down the street, 'cause I just don't like to deal with the mouth. So I think that's God's little funny way of saying, 'Ok, I'm gonna put you in the position' that I have to deal with somebody's mouth, because Qualeigh has to be suction and it's like, 'Oh my God! I never believed that I would.'

But I know that everything that happened was God. God put me in the position that that job was there. Because I wanted to just bring that application back, knowing that if I had brought that paper home, I would have never took it back, because I would be like, 'Oh well!' I got my retirement; they pay me to go to school, I ain't going to worry about it.' But then the lady was insistent. That was God. God played a role in everything that happened from that moment on. He had that purpose. I didn't know it. But God had laid it out for me. I was just faithful and I was obedient with it. So it got me the job, and then he moved me over there. And that kindled a fire in me that I did not think existed.

And then when I had the desire to bring him home, I talked myself out of it, you know, there's no way I can take care of him, I see what the nurses had to do, and then I had to change his diaper, then he had this green mucus stuff coming out of him, and I said, 'no way!'

But God saw something in my heart. God led me to take my children there. So, everything was produced by God. And then when we did make the decision as a family to get him, we were looking at finances. And it was like, 'there's no way!' With me not working now. We got our retirement. We got a house. We got these other kids and everything, and I take care of my mother, so there's no way, that we can do this.

God played! Right there! Because "BOOM," the lawyer was there! "BOOM," Consumer Services Board was there! And then they had the Money Follow the Person Program. I didn't know anything about it, but God put all these people in our lives to ensure that that transition went smoothly. And with the Money Follow the Person program, Qualeigh was the first one here, so his case worker had never done it before.

76

It worked out perfect. It was difficult the first two years because of the fact that I didn't go to work because I was not ready to walk away from him yet, to go back to work, and leave him for a long period of time. So then, things were not working out so well with getting personal care, somebody to come in and help me with him. So my days were long, taking care of him.

So I guess you can say that God has always positioned me in some situation to take me through something to let me know that I am capable of doing more than I think I can.

God gave me all that favor. I knew I had my favor so whenever God would put me in a position I always went to him for it. When he gives me something, especially something I don't think I can handle, I do it to the best of my abilities, and that was like with Qualeigh. I knew that it was for me to have Qualeigh, 'cause God has a mission for him. God has a purpose for him. There is something that God wants Qualeigh to do. And I'm a tool to help him accomplish what God wants him to do.

Because God would have never put him in my life if he didn't have a mission for him.

Chapter Twelve

RUBY MOORE
ATLANTA, GA

It wasn't just about evacuating facilities. It was about a picture of children having permanent homes and loving families.

I'm Ruby Moore. I'm the Executive Director of the Georgia Advocacy Office and we are the designated Protection and Advocacy System in Georgia for people with disabilities. Every state has a designated Protection and Advocacy System that we call P&As. The P&As are actually mandated by the congress, and we have enabling legislation that is very specific around our access authority to people with disabilities and in an effort to be an independent, external, safeguard to protect people from harm.

We literally have access to —in our routine monitoring— any place where people live, or work, or go to school that is funded as a service to people with disabilities. We have access immediately to people, and facilities and records, if there is probable cause of abuse and neglect, or if someone is in imminent threat or harm to their health or safety or well-being.

One of the things to know about our access authority as Protection and Advocacy Systems is that originally it came out of complaints by parents who had children who were in institutions and were appalled at the institutional condition and the abuse and neglect and harms that were happening.

That was back in the 70's, back in 1975 is when the P&A systems got formed. We've come full circle around access authority; the original intent continues today that people aren't safe in institutional settings, and while harm can happen in other places as well, we know that there's an increased vulnerability of people who are unnecessarily segregated, and particularly for children.

What we're trying to do through the Children's Freedom Initiative is bring home all of the children who are institutionalized in Georgia, and we're aiming to make sure the kids have permanent homes and loving families, and eventually to end the institutionalization of children altogether.

The Children's Freedom Initiative started when we discovered that there were over 140 children in nursing facilities in Georgia. First we just found a few kids. The Georgia Advocacy office and our routine monitoring as the protection advocacy system and through getting complaints from other people in the community about kids being neglected in facilities, we found that there were literally babies in nursing facilities. So we actually asked the question, 'how many children in Georgia are institutionalized?' And that turned out to be difficult to get the answer from the Department of Community Health.

Then, as a network of developmental disabilities organizations in Georgia, we have a federal mandate to work together; The Georgia Council on Developmental Disabilities, the Protection Advocacy System, which is the Georgia Advocacy Office, and then the two University Centers on Excellence in Developmental Disabilities; the Institute of Human Development and Disability at the University of Georgia and the Center for Leadership and Disability at Georgia State University

And so this was the issue that we raised, and everyone wanted to work on it, and we all have unique abilities as organizations. People were very excited about figuring out how many kids there were institutionalized and doing the work we needed to do to bring them home.

There were a group of national organizations, that were at the time, trying to pull together, what they called an alliance for full participation. It was around people with disabilities more fully participating in community life and living in the world. There was going to be a meeting in DC about each state having a team and coming to the meeting with an agenda. And so we had to get together and say, 'what's the agenda going to be; what are we going to bring forward?'

That's when we decided that we wanted to bring forward the issue of bringing home all the children who are institutionalized in Georgia, and we got together, and in preparation for that meeting, we started to think about, "who are the children; what did they need; where were they; what were the circumstances that they were found in; why were they institutionalized, and what might it take to bring the kids home?'

That's when we decided to have a summit and we brought together advocates and allies, kids with disabilities, their family members; we had doctors; we had behavioral psychologists, experts, Medicaid directors from outside of our state as well as state officials within the state; we brought legislators to the summit, because we wanted to craft a vision of 'what exactly are we trying to do here?'

It wasn't just about evacuating facilities. It was about a picture of children having permanent homes and loving families. We also wanted to get to the nitty-gritty details of what specifically are we trying to do; what are we not trying to do. So the summit really focused on what is home for anybody; for any child.

That was very powerful. We had legislators there sitting side by side with family members whose kids were at risk of institutionalization or who were institutionalized, and in some cases the kids were there. We were saying, 'what is a real home; What happens when children don't have real home; How are we going to bring the children home?'

We also brought people in from other states that have the same jobs as the state officials here, so for example if the Medicaid director said 'we can't do that'. Medicaid directors from other states who have been doing this for years said, 'Sure you can! This is what you need to do.'

We worked out a lot of, what I call the 'yeah-buts'. You know, what about the kids who are medically fragile? We had kids who were there who were considered to be medically fragile. We had doctors and developmental disabilities doctors there going, 'this is how you address the support needs of children who are medically fragile.' Here are

80

children who are medically fragile. Here's how we went about bringing them home. Here are some of the lessons from that that could help us on a broader scale. Same thing with kids who were considered to have significant behavioral support needs.

We had psychologists and we had people who knew how to develop family support systems and support any one child who might have behavioral difficulties or it be communicating in a way that's difficult for people to understand.

It was a very powerful summit, because the other piece we built in from the beginning was to have intentional developmental, protective, and corrective safeguards. So as we rolled out an initiative that would be very significantly formed, we were worried that wild perversions would be created.

For example; some people think, building a little orphanage is how you do this, you take kids out of a nursing facility and put them in a little orphanage, that somehow that's the community, or a little baby nursing facilities for kids coming home from the hospital,

well, 'you'll stay here for a few months'. Or group homes for children, I mean, there are all kinds of ways to do this wrong. So we started from the beginning making sure that we stood clear, stood firm, and that we were clear about what it is we're trying to do; what it is we are not trying to do, and making sure we did this well. That was the natural evolution of this.

Following the summit, we began bringing the children home; we were working hand in hand with the state to do that. We had allies within the state system as well as, outside of the state system. We've had local, national, even international support for what we're doing here. We had good media attention. We've had people helping to tell people's stories, which is very powerful in helping to build a consensus around what we're doing, as well as telling the story of what children need and how we go about making that happen.

We brought in a woman named Nancy Rosenau as a consultant who I've known forever, and who has done a lot of work in bringing children home. She's in Texas right now working in an organization called,

Every Child. I met her originally in Michigan, 20 years ago; a little group of us sued the state of Michigan because the commissioner of Mental Health and developmental disabilities actually asked us to sue him.

He said, 'I have 500 kids in nursing facilities and our legislature is not terribly interested or urgent about changing that situation.' A little group of us went and sued the state of Michigan and we brought home 500 kids, which was great. But Nancy was a General in the implementation Army maybe, because she was on the ground building a family support system so that it would actually be effective. Nancy came and consulted with the leadership of the Children's Freedom Initiative. We called it that name because that's what it is.

It was sort of doing like Disney does when they do the story boarding, they say, 'what are the words that actually describe what they're doing', and then you pick the most concise; smallest number of words to say what it is. We're freeing children from segregation and institutionalization and harm, and helping them to have the childhood that they need to have and deserve to have. There are some examples of states doing this right.

Vermont for example, has a good system of family support, and they've been very intentional about building local supports and what they call navigator systems to be very responsible, and flexible, and relevant to what the family's needs are, and to help the people to figure out how to navigate through service systems.

Massachusetts started fairly early on, at least in western Mass, where there were family leaders who insisted on being available to each other as peers and building a support system for families so that they could keep their children at home. There was a lot of early deinstitutionalization efforts in Massachusetts, and that prompted them along. Then there was a huge landmark case for EPSDT. Basically, it's part of the Medicaid law that says if a child needs something that is medically indicated, that they would get it. There was a huge case in Massachusetts. That was one recently, and so that prompts more family support as well.

In Ohio, they have community county-based systems and so they tend to be more flexible and responsive.

In Texas, I wouldn't tout the entire state as having good family support. Texas has some of the best examples of innovative approaches and has fairly recently passed permanency legislations. As the kids are institutionalized the state is mandated to begin planning for them to come home and to support them so that they don't become re-institutionalized.

The strategy for bringing the federal partners together within the Georgia Developmental Disabilities Network was in part around looking at the unique talents, and what each individual organization was uniquely positioned to do well.

There had to be a strategy for changing policy in the state, and so the Georgia Council on Developmental Disabilities was particularly strong in terms of working with the legislature and helping us craft coherent policy around bringing the children home. The children who were institutionalized were clearly misunderstood, so the true story of who they are and what they need, and sort of lifting the veil of confusion about what do children with disabilities need, which is the same question as what do children need.

Eric Jacobson is the Executive Director of the Georgia Council on the Developmental Disabilities, and when I came to Georgia, I think my first day on the job Eric called me and said, 'it's about homes, and friends, and jobs', and I said, 'OK, we're going to get along fine.' He is a kindred spirit, and he is very clear about those strategies needed to support people with DD across all age spans, and the Georgia Council is charged with doing planning and development and policy change for people of Developmental Disabilities in this state, and they do that very well.

Eric is particularly passionate about community organizing and figuring out—not just the formal systems of support and care for people but—how do you do more community-based, grass-roots organizing. He and the council have played a lead role, in working with the legislature when we were first starting off the initiative and we got House Resolution 633 passed. HR 633 urges state departments that have anything to do with children and disabilities, to work together to bring the children home.

The Georgia Council really played a key role in engaging the legislature; bringing legislators to the summit; making sure that people had the background information that they needed so that when we actually brought forth the resolution that it passed.

Dr. Zoe Stoneman is the Executive Director of the Institute of Human Development and Disability and she has been working on disability issues for decades, and has long been a champion for children. She has been a key player from the beginning in helping us be clear about what is known in the field, what has worked historically. The Institute on Human Development and Disability worked along with us at the Georgia Advocacy Office in telling the stories of the children who came home or who were at risk of institutionalization, and what it took to not have the children become institutionalized. This stood as the iconic stories of 'this is what it looks like when it's working, and when it's not working what are the corrective actions?'

The research capabilities of the University of Georgia are critical to all this because, it's not just about what's known in our field, and what's been the experience in Georgia. We're also trying to push the broader learning in our field about what children with disabilities need, what children and adults need, but in this particular case what children need.

Dr. Dan Crimmins came into Georgia and became the Executive Director of the second University Center for Excellence in Developmental Disabilities, specifically to help build the capacity for positive behavioral approaches for people with disabilities who have significant support needs, behaviorally. It was a huge piece that was missing and it was one of the primary reasons that children were institutionalized because those kinds of supports didn't exist.

The Center for Leadership and Disability at Georgia State University, the second University Center for Excellence for Developmental Disabilities, literally got formed at the request of people with disabilities in Georgia and our Developmental Disabilities Network, specifically to be a resource for families and others who were learning how to support people who had significant behavioral support needs. And so they've been a key player when people are saying 'this child can't come home because of his behavioral support needs', to have that clinical and programmatic and other expertise to be able to say 'oh we know how to do this', and to start building capacity first as a state to do this better.

Dan has been a very valuable asset to our team because it was a significant obstacle that we're trying to overcome that he has huge expertise in that area, and he's worked in other states doing that same work, and he has the clinical and programmatic expertise to be able to teach other people how to do it.

As the Georgia Advocacy Office, because we are the protection advocacy system and our primary mandate is to prevent abuse and neglect and death and harm for people with disabilities, we were uniquely positioned to be able to find the children, and to begin to bring both some pressure and resource to bare, to bring home each child, one person at a time.

It was nice too that everybody sort of checked their ego at the door, and said, 'this is way too important for any one of us to feel like we have to be the shining star, or take the credit, or always be the leader on this particular issue.'

We've handed that baton back and forth, as necessary, and we worked effectively as a collaborative of people, and we also had People First, which is a Statewide Self-Advocacy organization and the Statewide Independent Living Council involved from the beginning as well, because they know a lot about nursing facilities and transition and clearly people with disabilities being involved with every step, makes it more likely that you're not going to make obvious mistakes in recognizing who people are and what they need.

If other states were attempting to bring home children with disabilities who have been institutionalized, I think the very first thing and the most important thing is to figure out where their children are, look at the particular reasons that have been giving for children being institutionalized, understand and really spend some time with what the unique vulnerabilities might be of those particular children. Then think through what are some of the things that could go wrong in the process of transitioning the children, and build intentional safeguards to make sure that children aren't inadvertently harmed in the process.

I think it's important to have a political strategy, a legal strategy, the public education and research piece, and broad collaboration among people who understand children, who care about children, who understand how to support children and families to stay together and to not have children wind up back in the institution.

There needs to be a strategy for working with the state government systems to be able to direct or redirect or create the resources for family support. There needs to be, ultimately, a long term commitment to ending the institutionalization of children because going through all the work to bring the children home, only to have other children become institutionalized, is not what we're trying to do here.

Always keeping in mind that all children need the same things, all children need permanent loving homes; children need guidance; children need love and respect and families, and; they need to be a part of family life and community life, regardless of type or level of disabilities.

Chapter Thirteen

ERIC JACOBSON
ATLANTA, GA

*So, the idea of House Resolution 633 was to create a body that included
individuals representing state agencies, elected officials, families with
kids with developmental disabilities in institutions and
the developmental disabilities network.*

I'm Eric Jacobson, Executive Director of the Georgia Council on Developmental Disabilities. We are the Developmental Disabilities Council for the state of Georgia. Essentially our job is to create systems change through capacity building and advocacy so that people with developmental disabilities and their family members are more independent, productive, included and integrated into their communities and self-determining in their lives.

I think the first obstacle towards getting kids out of institutions is that there has to be leadership and a vision. Kids belong at home with families and that's the right thing to do. I think we're missing that. I think that once we have that agreement or that belief that that's where kids belong then the second barrier becomes that we don't necessarily have the infrastructure in place to provide quality supports in the community for kids or really for that matter anybody else that's in an institution. And so we need to use the resources; state resources, federal resources to build the infrastructures necessary to support kids in a manner that creates a quality of life.

When we created House Resolution 633 around the Children's Freedom Initiative we were looking back at what had happened with other efforts to close institutions like, for instance, the Olmstead plan; and one of the things that we recognized out of those early efforts was that unless there was a body in place that was created to hold the intent of that effort then it tended to fall apart. And so we said from the very beginning that we wanted to have some sort of oversight committee created around the Children's Freedom Initiative and moving kids out of institutions so that we could hold the state accountable for the goal of the Children's Freedom Initiative. So, the idea of House Resolution 633 was to create a body that included individuals representing state agencies, elected officials, families with kids with developmental disabilities in institutions and the Development Disabilities Network.

The Georgia Council on Developmental Disabilities has taken the role within the Children's Freedom Initiative as the public policy entity in terms of really pushing the resolution and working with legislators to get that resolution passed. We helped write the resolution and working with legislators got it passed through the General Assembly. Our role really is to be involved down at the state capitol during the legislative session and pushing legislation not only around children's issues but really all issues concerning people with disabilities. Pat Nobbie who is the Deputy Director at the Georgia Council on Developmental Disabilities was really the lead staff person in working with legislators to get HR 633 passed.

Because the Georgia Council on Developmental Disabilities is a state agency and we receive federal dollars, we don't lobby. Pat Nobbie is in charge of public policy and so her role is to work with legislators to help them understand the policies and implications of issues that are impacting people with developmental disabilities and their families. She is educating legislators, she's working with them on legislation, and she's able to mold policy that enhances people's lives and hopefully protects them from bad policy decisions.

For the first part we were able to get some of the state agencies to come to the table and even some of the legislators to come to the table and help us think through what needed to take place, but that didn't last very long. We were able to get representatives from the Department of Behavioral Health and Developmental Disabilities and their previous incarnations but really, part of the problem was that the Department of

Community Health was not at the table, Department of Juvenile Justice was not at the table, Department of Education was sporadically at the table. Each of those agencies has a part in helping kids come home. They have a program, they have money, they have resources in helping kids be supported in families and without them at the table and without them being a part of the conversation it really made it difficult to proceed. We were able to proceed as a DD network and to keep the conversation going but it was difficult without them at the table.

The DD Council, the Protection Advocacy Agency, the University Centers for Excellence in Disabilities, we've become in essence the oversight committee with occasional participation from other agencies. We meet on a monthly basis and we're talking about the issues that are important and how we can keep this thing moving forward as we move into the future.

Some of the agencies continue to play "behind the scenes" roles and so for instance, the Department for Behavioral Health and Developmental Disabilities has been instrumental in working with the DD network to help move kids home. Leadership and vision from the highest level is the obstacle that keeps kids from moving out of institutions. I think that if either the new commissioners that are coming on board with the new election or the governor himself said, "This is a priority. I want my representatives at the table, having a conversation about what it is we need to make sure that kids come home," then that would happen.

If other states wanted to replicate a Children's Freedom Initiative like Georgia's, first they must bring together that DD network, to make sure that the protection advocacy agency and the university centers and the DD Council are on board and that doesn't always happen in every state. This is an issue that could be used to bring those folks together. Once you do that, you're able to put some exposure to the issue. You can become successful at making this an important part of what's happening in your state. The idea that kids are living in institutions and the need to bring people home is and idea that we can all come together around. There shouldn't be any political philosophies that are keeping this from happening, it's really about the desire to say that in this country, in this world, in this state, no child should be in an institution and every child should be at home with a loving family and I think that that philosophy and that network being brought together can be successful in any state.

Chapter Fourteen

LES WAGNER
COLUMBIA, MO

*We do know this that for special needs infants and toddlers, physical
therapy, speech therapy, developmental interventions in a carefully
coordinated plan with knowledgeable physicians and pediatric therapists
can not only provide the opportunity for a child to talk sooner or walk
better but it may change the course the severity of the disability for the
rest of their life and their dependency on society.*

I'm Les Wagner I'm the executive director here at Boone Co. Family Resources. Boone Co. Family Resources is a local government program of services and support for persons with developmental disabilities and their families.

Well, the original idea 35 years ago was that we would have group homes. But it wasn't long after we established our first group home, which had a teaching emphasis, teaching people to be as self reliant and independent as possible. We realized that the vast majority of people were not going to need a group home. With the right kind of teaching and training support and developmental experiences the vast amount of people with developmental disabilities were going to live with their families and in the community and so while we continued to develop residential programs we had a big shift and we began to support families to have someone with special needs living with them.

Well I come from a long family of people who've been involved in working for people with disabilities. My grandfather was appointed by the governor to run an asylum. Then my father did this work before me and fortunately my son is involved in the same work. It is something our family believes is really important that community support those with disabilities and those families.

Well when we started the family support program 20 years ago it became the first nationally accredited family support program in the country. At that time the emphasis was on appropriations of money for institutions and facility based programs and of course those types of entities are well organized, they generally have trade associations. They employ people to lobby and represent them in the appropriations process.

The allocation of public resources is a political process. The nursing facilities, residential care facilities and other types of facility based programs are visible to legislators—they know where they are at—they are down the street in that big brick building with the blue façade on it. And I know who works there because they are part of an association that comes down and buys lunch for the legislators. Children that are living with families are living in dispersed neighborhoods. They live in homes that don't look any different than anybody else's home. They frequently are isolated, and unaware that even in the same neighborhood there are other persons with special needs. And so they are not as well organized there not as politically active and don't tell their story as well in the allocation of public resources as facility based programs.

Families with disabilities they never know when a disability is going to come to the door of any family that has kids. And when it does they are generally not expecting it. Not prepared and presented with challenges that will test their character and their resolve. And thinking about appropriations to support their family generally isn't first and foremost in their minds. They are living a day to day series of challenges. Missouri still has issues with respect to how much money we are going to spend on public institutions verses supporting families and helping people live successfully in their community.

Well we try to support families to meet the responsibilities they have got. Boone County Resources objective is to enable families to meet their responsibilities and not place their children in out of home placements. There are some circumstances where even with the best of support at the right time, specialized care facilities are what's needed. But the vast majority of the time, families that get what they need at the right time can be successful at meeting the special challenges they have and that's been our experience. They want folks to live with them to grow up with their brothers and sisters, and it's important to support families cause these families are at risk of divorce, greater risk of divorce. They're at greater risk of abuse and neglect of their child with special care responsibilities and behavior problems if they don't know how to handle them properly. The brothers and sisters of children with disabilities are at greater risk of referral to juvenile court and having school problems. So it's important for society no matter what your political persuasion to allocate resources to help these families meet those challenges successfully.

Well Kim and Brock are a great story because Brock is a teenager now but our agency has been helping that family for a number of years. Kimbal is a guy whose son developed a metabolic disorder, which affected his cognitive functioning, and his physical functioning and resulted in limitations that they didn't anticipate. But Kimbal is very committed to his son and he's hung in there. He has been the beneficiary of supports that were adequately funded by the government, state, county and federal resources that have been used to provide him with respite care, with personal assistance, with therapies and he can tell that story in his own words but the result is that his son lives with him today. And they're looking forward to a bright future in the community.

Families that have folks with disabilities that are children frequently can't just use the 14 or 15 year old babysitter in the neighborhood that other families use. They need someone who has experience with the care needs of that particular child with special challenges. And that's not easy to come by and you can't just necessarily pay them the ordinary babysitter wage. So respite programs identify people who receive training and experience in caring for people with special needs and then it gives the family a break. They are on point more so than the ordinary family and we all know the importance of ordinary families taking time to be together as a couple when they are not faced with the constant challenges of caring for children, with special needs children it's a more exaggerated situation so the break is all the more important.

Well we've been focusing upon individually planned person centered family support for over 20 years now. And when disabilities come they come in many forms. It may be a special needs baby that is born and you learn about it in the neo-natal clinic at the hospital. It may be a child that's born and they develop autism in early childhood. It may be a child that has an accident or a disease, an automobile accident at the age of 16 and so the types of packages and support they need vary depending on what their circumstances are. We do know this that for special needs infants and toddlers, physical therapy, speech therapy, developmental interventions in a carefully coordinated plan with knowledgeable physicians and pediatric therapists can not only provide the opportunity for a child to talk sooner or walk better but it may change the course, the severity of the disability for the rest of their life and their dependency on society. We do know that if it's an accident that happens in childhood that these are terribly stressful events for families and we know that one of the most important things perhaps the most important things that will determine whether the child will be placed out of the home or grow up with her brothers and sisters is whether or not the families believe they're going to be successful in meeting these challenges. And we do know that if they get the right supports at the right time, respite care, personal assistance, therapies job training, practical living skills training for the child so that they see that this child is becoming more independent and self reliant, then they have hope, they have optimism about their ability to meet the challenges that they never expected but that they think they're gonna get through. And if they believe they can get through them they persevere.

Well, with 20 years experience working focusing on nationally accredited family supports we've had some outcomes that we've hoped for but actually seen. It's not speculation as to whether or not we get people what they need when they need it. That as a population perhaps more of them will grow up with brothers and sisters. We know that that's the case. We know that the divorce rate improves. We know of families anecdotally of them statistically staying together. We know that more people are living with a relative, that there's a decrease in foster home placements, decrease in nursing home placements, decrease in group home placements and other benefits that as they grow to adulthood more people establish personal residences, successfully and more people get jobs successfully if you give them the right kind of support in there developmental years in their natural home.

Chapter Fifteen

MARK SATTERWHITE
HARRISBURG, MO

My understanding is that he lived his life in bed and just wasted away and eventually died of pneumonia at the institution. The only time I saw him was in his coffin at his funeral.

I'm from Harrisburg Missouri which is near Columbia Missouri. I work for an agency in Columbia Missouri called Boon County Family Resources. We provide services to people with developmental disabilities who live with their families or in the communities; on their own. We believe strongly in getting the support out to families that enables them to stay together in their natural homes and we feel strongly about including people with developmental disabilities in community life; in regular life.

My title at work is Director of Life and Work Connections, and the program I direct focuses primarily on kids who are transitioning to adult life. We provide life's skills training and work skills training to prepare them for adult life; integrated community life.

And we also provide life's skills training to adults who live with their families and aspire to live on their own in a more independent setting.

That's my primary role at work. I also serve as an advisor for the local People First chapter and I am involved with the Arc of Missouri which is another advocacy group for people with developmental disabilities.

Well, People First is an organization composed of people with developmental disabilities. It exists for them, and it's a self advocacy organization. They network with each other and support each other and advocating for the inclusion of people with developmental disabilities in regular life. People First is a civil rights movement. It's all about getting

96

away from segregation of people with developmental disabilities and moving toward including them in their communities.

Felons are institutionalized. People who committed no crime should not be institutionalized, and in a nutshell, that is the view of People First.

Putting people in an institution and segregating them from society is degrading; it degrades them as people who are not people first; they're labeled first as people who can't be in the community and must be institutionalized. That's how we treat felons.

The ARC of Missouri is not headquartered. It's a grassroots organization of people from across the state, and so the officers of the organization live in different parts of the state and we get together; the board meets periodically, and that constitutes the core organization.

That organization is focused on getting families involved in advocating for supports and services that they need in the natural home and community. There is a waiting list for services for five thousand people in Missouri. Five thousand people in Missouri with developmental disabilities get no supports and services.

None of those five thousand that I'm aware of is waiting for institutional placement. These are families who are struggling with extraordinary responsibilities. The ARC advocates that these families deserve supports and services and natural homes and communities.

One of our approaches to the lack of funding that results in lack of supports and services for them, is to advocate for the closure of institutions — not only because we feel that it's wrong to segregate people into institutions who committed no crime – but it's also economically smart. Millions are poured in to serving people in institutions. We know that it's cheaper for taxpayers to support people in the community even if they need 24/7, around the clock, one-on-one supervision.

Through the Medicaid Home and Community-Based Waiver, federal funds are available to — as matched — the state funds to supporting people in their natural homes and communities as an alternative to institutional care.

In Missouri we call our institutions...public institutions for people with developmental disabilities "habilitation centers," their classified under Medicaid as Intermediate Care Facilities for the Mentally Retarded [Excuse my use of that term]. And so, home and community-based waiver funds, that's what people are waiting for; that's what the five thousand people are waiting for.

Families would have services like personal assistance: a personal assistant to come in and help care for their family member, or a respite care provider to augment parental support.

Families supporting people with intensive needs are at risk for breaking up.

Through the Medicaid Waiver, services and supports that are very expensive would be affordable because federal funds through the waiver would help pay for them. Services like specialized equipment and medical supplies that people with physical disabilities and intensive medical care needs, require those things would become more affordable for families.

Caregivers could come into the home and augment parental supports and help provide relief to families who face extra ordinary responsibilities and also risks for breaking up. I'm personally aware of families whose children have intensive support needs and mom or dad says, "I'm done; I'm leaving!" These are people on the waiting list and haven't been able to get access to the waiver and affordable services and supports.

I am personally aware of families who have divorced; couples who have divorced when mom or dad can no longer take the stress of the lack of support, and yet institution just doesn't seem to be a consideration for contemporary families. What they want is support in their homes and communities and our hope (when I say "our hope," I mean the hope of advocates in Missouri hope) that these kinds of outcomes can be avoided; divorce can be avoided, segregation of people into placement settings outside the natural home wouldn't have to happen.

My personal story; my first connection with disability happened last century. My brother was born in the late 1950s, I think, 1955 he was

98

born, and in the 1950s, last century, institutional care was the going model for supporting people with developmental disabilities; for supporting children and the physicians advised my parents that his needs were so intensive; his disability so severe, that he would require care in an institution. They moved him to a place called, I believe it was called, the St. Louis State School and Hospital on Bellfountain road in St. Louis and that's where he lived and died; he died at a young age. He died in 1966, and I never knew him and he never knew me, so as siblings we were completely separate, which is very unnatural for families, and I am honored to be involved in civil rights movement for people with developmental disabilities that includes them in the community. I am very happy that supports and services, today, are available as alternatives to institutional care for children.

I wish I had known my brother and I wish he had known me. I don't think that that's something that was possible for us last century, but it is possible in this century today, for contemporary siblings to know each other, to grow up together, and you know, that's my hope for today.

It's fulfilling to be involved with an agency that supports families and keep families together and also, I'm proud to be involved in the advocacy movement for people with developmental disabilities.

My mother and father felt like really there was no alternative. They were planning to have children; they have three other children and Michael; my brother, was the first born in the family and the doctor told them that his needs were so intensive that my mother wouldn't be able to care for any additional children.

Her 24 hours would be wrapped up with caring for him. I'm not sure of his exact diagnosis, but I know that he was blind. I know that he has spasticity to the extent that he could not walk, and he basically—my understanding is that he lived his life in bed and just wasted away and eventually died of pneumonia at the institution.

The only time I saw him was in his coffin at his funeral.

I know that, I used to ask my parents...I was five when he died, but I remember vividly his funeral. Prior to his death though, I used to ask my parents about my brother, and I would ask if I could go see him and they told me that they did not want me to see him because they thought I would be traumatized by the environment where he lived.

My mother became involved in the field of developmental disabilities back in the 1970s. In the 70s, a lot of things happened in the field of developmental disabilities. We started to think about services and supports. We started to think in terms of keeping families together and providing those services and supports in the home so that families could be together and get the support they need, and so that children wouldn't have to be separated from their families and institutionalized.

Things started to shift, big time in the 70s, toward the community inclusion of people with developmental disabilities. Different states moved at different paces. In Missouri, we still have six publicly supported institutions for people with developmental disabilities. There is one in Nevada. There's one in Marshall. One in Higgensville; Bellfountain in St. Louis. There's another one in St. Louis. One in the Kansas City area.

Well, I know that recently in Nevada, plans that were inspired by cost savings were made to close that institution and they also planned to convert that...close the big building, convert it to a campus of smaller building, and to put small groups of people in each of those buildings.

The state, for budgetary reasons, made the decision to close the Nevada Habilitation Center. The solution to cost savings they were proposing was to downsizing the institution from a big building with lots of people to a campus of smaller building with lots of people, still separated from the community. The advocacy community was kind of in an uproar. We didn't see that as the closure of an institution and including people in the community so much as we saw them downsizing. Their plan was to access home and community-based waiver funding to support those people in the smaller homes, and their rational was "these were more home-like," than the institution.

The Centers for Medicare and Medicaid services, which is the Medicaid authority, the federal Medicaid authority disallowed that plan and now the state plans to close the Nevada Habilitation Center and move its residence into the community. We see that as a positive step toward Missouri's future, and including people with developmental disabilities in their communities.

I think there were department mental health officials and legislators who realized that that was a cost savings mechanism and I think they moved forward and in a well-intentioned manner, but it defies the principle upon which home and community-based waiver funds are made available. They're made available as alternatives to institutional care and this was the conversion of an institutional to an institutional campus.

So the federal government ruled that it was inappropriate to use home and community-based funds for that purpose.

I think nursing homes and other types of institutions, including habilitation centers for people with developmental disabilities have organized lobbies and paid lobbyists in many cases, not the habilitation centers themselves, but they have support groups, have center parents for example, and guardians who enlist lobbyists to advocate at the capitol.

On the other side, largest portion of advocates in Missouri who consist of families trying to support their kids in the home and in need of services, are not as well organized as they should be. They have extraordinary responsibilities. They don't have the time to compete with paid lobbyists for other kinds of institutions that we feel like, need to go away.

We feel that resources and when I say "we," I'm talking about me as an individual, and I'm talking about ARC, and I'm talking about People First, we feel that expensive resources that goes toward institutionalizing people should be devoted to community-based supports and services.

Chapter Sixteen

REBECCA MCCLANAHAN
SULLIVAN COUNTY, MISSOURI

And the concern that anyone would have of an institutional setting is that it prevents them from having that richness of experience that improves the quality of life for anyone whether they are young or not. But certainly the young need that richness of experience in order to develop as normally as possible.

My name is Rebecca McClanahn and I am the house representative in state district 2 in Missouri. And I represent the people of Adair Putman and a portion of Sullivan County here in North Missouri. Before I was in the legislature I spent 30 years as a registered nurse and as a nursing professor at Truman State University in Kirkland, Missouri. And my specialty in nursing is psychiatric mental health nursing. So I had the opportunity to work with young nursing students in a variety of mental health settings.

Here in Missouri the state actually still runs a number of facilities that are state run facilities with state employees that are habilitation centers. And so we have a number of habilitation centers around the state. The number of beds in those facilities has actuality decreased over a number of years, but we still have large facilities around the state. And so as other states have transitioned to closing all habilitation centers and focused on community based housing we just have not done that kind of process here in Missouri. Although we've made some progress, I believe we still have a long way to go.

I was able to visit that Nevada Habilitation Center just over a year ago. And I was with another registered nurse that's also a member of the Missouri House of Representatives and the two of us had just asked the department to help us tour many of the facilities around the state. And we toured many psychiatric facilities as well as habilitation centers. And so with the opportunity to visit the Nevada habilitation center, I was struck with the age of the buildings, the buildings are quite old.

The age of the buildings and just clearly the institutional feel congregate setting, if you will. There were large groups of individuals living together. And although there is some effort to split up into smaller areas where only few people were living that would at least simulate a home setting, it clearly was still in an institutional setting with very long hallways and very old buildings and on a campus that is set aside from the rest of the community. So the clear separation from the rest of the community and it was quite obvious too.

Well, we all want to live in a community, I think we all want that interest and to be able to move around our community unfettered in a way that meets our needs and none of us sees ourselves living in an institution. And that separates people from the community that creates stigma. That creates separation that emphasizes difference. It doesn't celebrate them certainly. It emphasizes how different people are with special needs. I think it really reinforces some of that stigma or prejudice that separates people rather than brings them together. And in an institutional setting too, many of the decisions are made for a person; you just have to go along with the program. And that's the way institutions work. And so I think it limits individuality and limits individual freedom. I was able to speak with a young man that had lived at the Nevada Habilitation Center for some time. And I believe at the age of 21 he began the effort to try to leave the facility and live in an integrated community setting; and it took a while, I'm not remembering the details of how long it took him to transition in to more home like atmosphere his own individual apartment, but he talked about the freedoms and the ah, privacy that he had when he was able to move into his own setting. To be able to listen to the music he wanted to and play video games as a young man perhaps want to do and the ability to sleep in in the morning or stay up late at night, all of those choices were really important to him. Being able to watch the channel on TV that he wanted to chose rather than watching what was chosen for him was really, really important to him.

When a person lives in a congregate care setting just the risk to infections, the common cold or flu is so much more common in that setting when people live with large groups of people. A person with a disability maybe particularly vulnerable to infections. The risk of pneumonia would be common in someone that has some structural difference that affects their posture. So in congregate care setting where there may be other people that have colds or flu, something that I might experience as a bad cold, and what I might call a chest cold, would be a common term, might actually be influenza. And with a person that's particularly vulnerable that influenza might be a really serious illness and perhaps put their life at risk. So the exposure to that in a congregate care setting would be a particular risk.

I certainly have seen options here in our own community here in Kirksville for care outside of institutions and we have many independents supported living homes in the community where there's staff support anywhere from a few hours a week to perhaps 24/7, staff supervision, but it's still a home setting. It's integrated in a community, it has a yard and sidewalks and perhaps a deck and a front stoop with a basket of flowers; all of those things that make a house a home. But I visited homes that are here in our community where persons with severe disabilities are able to be maintained with staff support in much the way they would in an institutional setting but it's in a home setting and has all of the advantages of a home setting.

So a parent that doesn't have that, though, they don't have that, either they are in a community that is so rural that that's not available that a provider can't reach them or they are in a state in which there's a waiver and there's a waiting list for that. What would you say to that parent?

Well the waiting list is a real struggle for us in Missouri we have thousands of people on our waiting list for home and community based services it's a real concern, a continual concern to those of us in the Missouri legislature especially those of us that are a member of the community. The appropriations community makes decisions about the budget for the Department of Mental Health. And so that is a real problem. I think, here in Missouri a person must achieve a certain score in their assessment in order to qualify for the services that are available because those services are limited. I really believe we need to push for this concept and parents should push for the concept, "The Money Follows the Person," so if there is money for institutional care then that money should be spent on that person in a community based setting. And if there are funds that could be expended then we should be able to find people to do the coordination of care. Here in this county, in Adair County we actually have what we call an SB40 board, it's based on Senate Bill 40 was passed a few years ago and that allowed the citizens, voters to vote to tax ourselves using a mil tax in order to provide additional services here in the county and so we are able to support additional case managers.

So a number of counties in Missouri have chosen to do that. And Adair County has chosen to do that. And so we are able to support additional disability services here in the county. And so we have actually taken over case some management services that were formerly done by state employees in Missouri and we are able to provide those to our citizens here in this county.

Well as a member of the appropriations committee in the House of Representatives we work on the budget for the department of mental health. I also happen to be on the budget committee in House of Representatives so through that budgetary process our obligation is to fund state services. So when we have institutions that are in place they, find it necessary to fund that care. And it makes it very difficult to shift money from institutional care, shift to a different process. So it's just even the complexity of the budget process itself, it tends to perpetuate itself, I believe. So it takes really intentional planning and a careful focus to try to shift money to different programming. You know we are in difficult times, we are in a budget crunch and cash flow is a problem and so we're looking for ways of cutting the budget. We're required by our Missouri constitution to balance the budget. So we are looking for places to cut and it seems like that first place we go is home and community based services. Because we have this fundamental obligation to fund care that we provide and the institutions for which we are responsible for in this state. And so I think part of that is just the challenges of the budget process and trying to find places to trim what could be considered discretionary spending. When from the point of view of a family or a person with a disability it's not discretionary at all, it's essential services.

I'm confident that institutional care or nursing facility placement would affect the development of a person with disabilities much as it would so many things effect the normal development of a child. And children without a disability need a rich experience with many stimuli and the opportunity to explore their world and a child with disabilities would need that opportunity as well and might even need additional assistance in experiencing just stimulating their senses in order grow and develop and learn. I had the opportunity of visiting a home here in Kirksville and it's actually managed by a local not for profit group and it's a home that's integrated into a community and three individuals with severe disabilities are supported in that home. And when I visited, there were pumpkin muffins in the oven. And I enjoyed the sensation and aroma of the pumpkin muffins. And that has come to represent for me the rich experience one can have in the home setting. So I've begun to say everyone should have the pumpkin muffin. And we all want that for our lives we want a rich sensory environment. And to make choices that give us that exposure. And the concern that anyone would have of an institutional setting is that it prevents them from having that richness of experience that improves the quality of life for anyone whether they are young or not. But certainly the young need that richness of experience in order to develop as normally as possible.

I would hope that we could move in Missouri away from institutional care to more community based care and I'd like to use the term integrated community based care that is integrated into a neighborhood, integrated into a home as much as possible. And I have some concerns that on two of our habilitation facilities. There is actually new building occurring on those campuses, group homes. So they will be smaller facilities but they will still be on a campus that has historically been known as a place where people have been set apart and prevented from integration in to society. And we're making a significant financial investment in Missouri—millions of dollars will be spent in the next couple of years building group homes on campuses, when I believe we could be spending that money to focus on more community based settings and perhaps even save money by doing an investment off of those campuses. What I fear is that with this new investment in buildings, brick and mortar on those campuses I fear that we are committing ourselves to more institutional based care for the next 30 years when from my point of view that type of care is already outdated. It is a mode of care whose time has passed. And we should be moving aggressively to integrated care. People that talk to me about these issues tell me that for every person receiving institutional care in the state of Missouri they have a twin that is receiving integrated community base care. So there is not a single person that is being cared for in the state of Missouri at this point that could not be residing in community based setting. and I would hope that we could have a fundamental shift in thinking here in Missouri that we could move in that direction instead of investing in outmoded treatment that doesn't respect the individual rights and the individual liberties and the diversity of the person and does not contribute as much to the quality of life as it could.

Chapter Seventeen

RISHI AGRAWAL
CHICAGO, IL

Instead of having ideological battles as to which is better, homecare versus institutional care, the more important thing to do is to try to make sure that families don't feel like they have to place their children out of home just because of a lack of services in the community.

I'm a pediatrician at La Rabida Children's Hospital. I take care of many children who have physical disabilities, as well as children who require the assistance of medical technologies in order to survive. My experience has been that there is quite a bit of variation between those nursing homes, but I would say that there's no substitute for a loving family.

The advantages of keeping children with disabilities in their home are several: one is that they have proximity to their family and their siblings, the other is that it keeps them within society and so it doesn't become a situation where society can say, "You can just go off and be hidden." I think that that has broader benefits in terms of society's acceptance of people with disabilities that they're in our schools; you see them when they're going shopping, and that they're not hidden from the population, because in society if we're going to enhance the experience for our most vulnerable citizens, then keeping them hidden is not the best way to do that.

A loving home is very healthy because you have constant stimulation from a parent who watches over the child and gives them a fair amount of attention. Now of course, not all parents are able to do that, but you have a situation where a child can be watched over and can be advocated for constantly, and that is a unique facet of being in a home environment.

I think that this comes down to children with disabilities, and making sure that their rights are respected no matter if they're in the home environment or institutional care environment.

Some children do okay in institutional settings, but you do have some scenarios, particularly with some facilities where there certainly is an element of neglect that goes on and I think that in any way that we can try to improve the care for these children, whether they are in facilities or at home, is really important.

So the reason that many children are at risk or end up in institutional care is, in part, because of the success of medicine; we're able to keep more kids alive today than we previously were because of new technologies. We able to keep kids alive with feeding tubes and breathing tubs and ventilators, and that was something that just didn't happen in the past. So we have more capability of keeping these children alive. So that's one reason that it has become more difficult. Some of the kids just weren't around and surviving before twenty or thirty years ago.

So the other trend that we have is that parents are asked to do a lot more when they take care of these children. There have been steady cut backs in the amount of services that will be provided.

Prior to the 1980s many children who had severe disabilities and who needed medical technologies in order to survive were kept in hospitals or in institutions.

There was a girl name Katie Becket who argued that if the government was going to pay for services in a hospital and they could do the care at home, why not give them that money in order to provide the necessary care at home.

At that time an exception was made for the federal rules regarding services, and Katie Becket was allowed to stay in the home. Eventually the law was amended to allow states to develop waiver programs: and what waiver means is that the regular rules of Medicaid are amended so that states could create programs that serve a particular population.

So there are a number of programs that could help children stay at home, and we are advocating in order to keep making these programs more robust so that they suit the needs of families.

The problem is that they're not necessarily flexible for the needs of the families. They have to have a certain number of hours of nursing within a certain week; within a certain period of time and you cannot use more hours in one week, versus another week. The payment rates to the nurses are much lower than they are to nurses in a hospital setting.

There are many ways that if we were flexible would be a way that the dollars were allocated, that we could meet the needs of families who want to keep their children at home.

Some of the things that I'd like to see would be if a family lives in an area which doesn't have many nurses who lives close to them that perhaps nurses could get mileage reimbursement to get to their home. We find that with the higher cost of gas that some nurses just aren't willing to travel, particularly to rural areas.

I would like to see that if there is a particularly complex; very challenging child to take care of that the reimbursement structure reflects the increased needs of that child, so that you don't have situations where the nurses are drawn towards the least complex cases, and that the children who have the highest levels of need, they have the hardest time getting access to the home nursing resources.

The children who have the highest levels of need are at risk because, first of all, their medical needs are so high, but then also because it's harder to find nurses who are skilled and are willing to take care of them especially when the pay rates for the nurses are so much lower than those skilled nurses could earn in a hospital setting.

The tragedy of this is that it's often more expensive to care for these children in a hospital or in an institutional care setting. If these programs were a little bit more flexible in how they allocated their resources, and they said, "OK, what is it going to take within the budget that we have in order to keep these kids at home?" I think that they could keep more of them with their families, and I think that that would be a great thing because there's really no substitute for a loving family in terms of enhancing the developmental and physical outcome of children who has such challenges.

Instead of having ideological battles as to which is better, homecare versus institutional care, the more important thing to do is to try to make sure that families don't feel like they have to place their children out of home just because of a lack of services in the community; that our community services maximize the probability that a family will be able to keep their children at home, and that means being flexible.

If there is one word that I would say is really important is "flexibility" because these are complex situations. The situations are often as complicated as the family, the child's medical circumstances.

So in order to do the things that we need in order to keep them at home, we have to think a little bit outside the box in terms of the services we provide. That's why I favor a more global budgeting system.

I think we should take a holistic view of what the family needs within a certain budget; how can we meet those needs and then go from there. One size does not fit all, and so that would be a key message, I think, going forward.

Chapter Eighteen

AMBER SMOCK
CHICAGO, IL

*We're the kind of community that relies on the idea that anyone can join
the disability community at anytime, so we fight for
everyone because we're everywhere.*

At the Chicago Center for Independent Living, Access Living works
to integrate people with disabilities in the communities at all levels, that
include children Living Children with Disabilities and what we do is we
work to empower people by teaching them self advocacy skills.

We provide services in advocacy that support people with disabilities
and being able to integrate in the communities at all levels; being able to
stay at home; being able to go to school; being able to get a job; be able
to be full human beings in the city that we live in.

Access Living does a couple of different things: one is that we
provide de-institutionalization services to support people with disabilities
who currently live in nursing homes to move into their own homes. We
also provide support groups and peers mentoring for people so that they
understand what it's like to live in the community from someone who's
been there before.

For children with disabilities we provide support for mothers and
young people with disabilities who understand what it's like to be young
and trying to make their own decisions and also how to deal with their
families. Some families are very supportive, but young people have to
learn to make their own way as well.

Families will find us through word-of-mouth. They will also find us
through advocacy; support that they experience when they're trying to
deal with the problem for the child. So quite often what happens is that
families find us when they call Access Living because they hear, "Oh!

Access Living knows how to work with schools and IEPs." And so what we'll do is, is we'll spend and hour or two talking with them, finding out what's going on with the IEP, what is the school providing, what is the school not providing, what types of transitional support are you receiving and we'll go from there. Generally the experiences are positive, so they'll keep talking it up.

When families are advocating for improved educational services for students with disabilities, one thing that is often overlooked, is whether they're living in the place where they want to be living for the next ten to fifteen years. Usually IEPs don't cover whether a child has a plan to live with the family or an institution after they finish High School. At that point, families often find—because there is no preparation—that they're at a loss as to what to do, and that's a pressure point where you're gonna find someone whose placed in an institution. And nobody gets prepared.

There are actually boxes on the IEPs that ask whether or not the family has been trained in personal attendant services and state services...there's actually a box that says that, but it's actually left unchecked. Nobody actually goes over that with them. So to be honest, I feel that when families face that cliff of graduation, and they reach the child's final year of high school, they say, "Well, it looks like Billy's gonna graduate in June; Oh, what are we gonna do?" And at that point, what we find is that people start calling us trying to ask, "Is there some kind of day program that my child can participate in because we have to work all day; so we can't stay at home taking care of Billy, because the school used to do that and we have to make money so we can eat?"

So at that point, people start saying, "Hey, there's a problem, what are we gonna do?" And I think, unless they're connected with the Social Services Agency, they are not going to know automatically that there is another choice than the nursing facilities. The nursing facilities industry sells itself very well. Social Services don't have a marketing campaign.

So I think that it's that last year of high school that turns out to be a period of confusion and fear, and a point where people find themselves resorting to what they never thought they would do. In the final year of high school when parents start looking at what they're going to do with the child when they graduate, what happens is you have a family who is stressed out, they're fearful, and they don't know their option, and that's the point at which the nursing home marketing campaign really can pickup and get that family's ear.

What happens is the nursing home will sell themselves, and say "Hey, this is a great place where your child will be taken care of." They will be supportive. They will go out; they'll have people that care about them, and it sounds like a really great opportunity. The Social Services Agency don't have a marketing campaign like that. They don't have enough money to go out to every family in the city and say "Hey, we can help you have your child live at home with you just like you've been doing."

If a parent calls Access Living at that critical point before high school graduation and say: "I have a child with a severe disability, and I don't know what I'm gonna do with them when they graduate high school. School has always been there to take care of them throughout the day. Maybe there's a day program that you know about?"

What Access Living is going to say is:

"Well, we have programs that support self-advocacy and independent living skills development if your child can take advantage of those. If your child can't take advantage of those, we can also help you to learn about the home services waiver, or about programs where your child could go for the day."

Without that kind of support; without somebody to hold your hand, that's when families start feeling like they're by themselves, and they don't have any options, and then they end up placing their child in an institution.

At various times I hear that the waiting list is very, very long; very long, and generally there is a few thousand people at a given point waiting for services from the state of Illinois. It depends on what disability you're talking about; if you're talking about somebody who has a developmental disability it may be different from someone who has a psychiatric disability. If your child had two kinds of disabilities, two

114

kinds of waivers may apply and the state may say you have to pick one. It gets complicated.

Without a waiver, poor kids don't have a chance; without a waiver, rich kids may get support; with a waiver, poor kids may have access to things like home care, programs, friends, opportunities, job development; without a waiver, they don't get any of that; rich children may have access to nurses; whatever the money can pay for. It really is about money.

So it's not fair that in the state of Illinois, poor kids have to stay at home and families have to lose jobs in order to take care of those children. It's not fair. We're one of the richest states in the country, and we're one of the worst states - if you're a child with a disability – to live in. The struggle for community integration in Illinois has been taking place for the last thirty years, and children are the last frontier, so what's been happening is advocates have been trying to make sure that adults get funded for services and support in the community, but children are left out of that every time because the legal rules are different for children, because you may have guardianship and also because of age.

Until we're able to find a way to make sure that children have the choice to live at home; that they have waivers or supports that they need, then the battle for real community integration is not going to be over. Many times outsiders who are not familiar with disability advocacy may ask a disability rights group, like Access Living. "Why were you so invested in fighting for the rights of people who are not your own children? These are not your children. These are not your family. They're not even, geographically, next door to you. Why do you bother fighting for the rights of these kids?"

My response is that, we are a community. We're not the kind of community that relies on being neighbors, physically.

We're the kind of community that relies on the idea that anyone can join the disability community at anytime, so we fight for everyone because we're everywhere.

What we consider a client of Access Living is not the people who come through our doors every day, its every single person with a disability who's in the Chicago area. That's who we fight for.

Chapter Nineteen

DONNA HARNETT
CHICAGO, IL

I got, I got it in a huge way. I wouldn't put my dog in half of these institutions. I got it that my son's worst day at home would be better than his best day in a place like some of these...

I was pregnant, 31 years old, went to all my doctor's appointments, did everything I was supposed to do, went into labor, it went south. I was in the wrong place at the wrong time. When he was initially born I was told that they weren't sure if he was going to make it or not and it was an hour-to-hour situation. Initially they said that maybe there was a 10 percent, 5 percent chance he would live for any length of time.

He had been in the pediatric intensive care unit for two and a half weeks. It was about when he was six weeks old I realized that there was something really, really wrong.

My gut told me there was a problem. He was having seizures and he had some of them right after he had come home and I had called the PICU saying I don't understand why would my son be shaking like this and they initially told me it was the drugs left over in his body. And I'm thinking there's no drugs with a half-life of a week and a half, two weeks so I didn't buy it. He had a MRI done and that's when the amount of damage became very apparent.

My son was born missing three quarters of his brain, although I did not find that out until a little bit after the fact, maybe about a couple of months. Where his brain should have been was filled with spinal fluid, he had Microcephaly, the technical term for his brain issue was Cystic Encephalomalacia, and also Cerebral Palsy; being the garbage can term that it is. He had reflux, he had seizures, there were multiple issues. He also had scarred lungs because of Meconium.

Martin was seizing all of the time, it was such abnormal brain activity between that and reflux he was screaming probably, easily 23 out of every 24 hours. It was non-stop. My son and I were apart maybe a grand total in a span of 14 years maybe a total of six weeks and initially there was a two week span of time after all the problems became apparent all the screaming I was so sleep-deprived that he did go to what was Misericordia South, when it existed. It was in the time period that I was able to get some sleep. It had been so bad that I had informed one of the social workers that I was on the verge of taking my son to an ER and leaving him there if I did not get help to take care of my son because in addition to not sleeping there's also things like the laundry, going shopping, cooking, these kinds of things. So my first goal was to get some help.

We were in a state of crisis and the thought did cross my mind to have him somewhere other than home for a short amount of time. And I of course, like many people knew, about nursing homes for elderly people and it just didn't seem like the right thing to do or something that I could live with, making that type of decision, so I needed help. I wanted respite. I heard about respite, I knew about this, non-specialized care that could help me keep it together. So, I got myself an advocate from Community Alternatives Unlimited and she wrote up a grant. At this point, my then husband was in and out of the picture, he basically didn't exist. She writes up the grant, she submits it to the state and nothing happens, and nothing happens, and then nothing happens. Then more of nothing happening so I finally called her and I'm like what's the story here, what is going on with this? "Well you might have to take some more drastic measures." Fine, what would those drastic measures be? She said, "You're gonna have to contact your elected officials and have a conversation with them about this." Thinking great, how am I gonna do this? So being a resident of the city of Chicago and knowing how all that works I contacted my alderman. Went in and talked to him and said, "I need to talk to my state senator, I need to talk to him directly, not an aide, this is important, I would not bother you if this was not important." Lo and behold, I got a call from my state senator and I explained the situation; that it was next to impossible to care for my son at home. I needed this help, the monies were available, we're a great candidate for it because it was determined at that time that my son, if he were not home with me, would be eligible to go into a SNF/PED – specialized nursing care facility for pediatrics.

So I got really frustrated cause then I didn't hear back from him. So I talked to the advocate. I had a game plan, and the game plan was this; it was actually going to save taxpayers money to fund me, to keep my son at home with the care that he needed. We're talking eight hours a day, five days a week. As taxpayers, even if nobody else cared about anything else, seems to me, as taxpayers, we might care where the tax money is going. It seems to me like a fiscally responsible kind of thing to do. So, I finally call my state senator's office back and I talk to I don't know, his receptionist. By then my advocate and I had phone numbers of the press and I was going to take this to the wall, so to speak. I explained to her something really needed to happen cause I said this is what's going to happen if we're not funded. If we don't get the money, I said, I will put my son into an institution and I will call, and I start listing out names of reporters I was gonna call, and I said really, this is gonna be embarrassing. Not gonna be embarrassing for me and my family, this'll be embarrassing for my elected officials.

She told me, "Well you shouldn't threaten like that" and I'm like hold on a second, I'm not playing here, this is not a threat. I'm giving you fair warning of exactly what I'm going to do if this thing does not get signed off on and if we do not get some help over here. This is a promise, not a threat and I was ready to do it. And the story goes she got off the phone, goes into his office, tells him I had called. He picks up the piece of paper, goes down the hall, goes into the office of whoever the head of that particular agency, threw it on the desk and said, "Sign this." And apparently the secretary tried to stop him and he just like marched in, threw it on the desk said sign it. She signed it, he grabbed it, I got a phone call back within five minutes said it had been signed. And what really struck me is this, why? Why does it take this kinda effort? Why? What is the problem with the system that I have to start off with making an appointment with an alderman in order to get to my state senator in order to get something to happen to keep my son at home? Crazy.

So then I went through the Partners and Policy making training here in Illinois and I did that when my son was a year and a half. I went through the training and I got to hear firsthand and meet people firsthand who talked about what life was like in an institution. I got, I got it in a huge way. I wouldn't put my dog in half of these institutions. I got it that my son's worst day at home would be better than his best day in a place like some of these...

My son being at home was the most important thing. My son transitioned out of the early intervention program here in Illinois at three years old. Then he went into the Chicago public schools. There was an inclusion bill that was in Springfield right around the same time. I had written testimony and one of the things I had pointed out when I went to the initial meeting with the IEP is that our local school had never had a child in a wheelchair before. Community, school, the connections that we have in life—we all as individuals learn so much about what is normal from our day-to-day interactions in our community. One of the reasons I so wanted Martin in his community, in his local school, it wasn't just about him. It was about other kids learning it was ok to be different. We don't all look the same. We're not all the same color. We're not all the same religion. Our families have different amounts of money. It had to do with how much more alike we really are than we are different and my son was more alike compared to the other children than he was different and that was really important. Because my son was at home, Martin has other siblings; he has brother who is a year and a half younger than him and then twin brothers who are then another year younger, their view of the world is so much bigger and so much different. They're not living in this little box. Their world is huge because as a result of having Martin in our life, in our day-to-day activities and being out in the community we also met other individuals in the disability community and my kids had interaction with these people. We used to go to the marches and protest. I would yank my kids out of school, to show them that it's really important to stand up for something. I can't think of anything really that's more important than that.

Chapter Twenty

DOROTHY ROSENTHAL
CHICAGO, IL

And the reward is going to be knowing that I did everything I could
possible do to help you find who you are and what you're going to be. I
will never ever have to look back and say I wish,
I should've, I could've...

I have opened my home up to children who have extra challenges. There's a need for it. It's not something one should take lightly. There should be homes for them because there are not a lot of parents that want to meet those challenges. But I think that once you do it is very rewarding. And the children are so loving and so appreciative.

Originally that was not my goal to take on a child with disabilities. I wanted to be a parent and found that biologically I couldn't reproduce so I thought I'll be a foster parent. That if a child became available I'd adopt that child. So originally it was not a special need, but I was registered, had taken the classes, had been participating for four years and I got a call that said they had a little boy, Cody, he had special needs. Then two years later they said we have, a little girl, Giani she has some special needs. And I thought, okay. I met those special needs with Cody; I think I can do it for her. I couldn't imagine not doing it. So I took her on; I thought if I say I can do this with Cody, I can do it with Giani. And I did it. So it wasn't a conscious thought but once it was presented to me as a, 'do you want this, and she has special needs' I couldn't imagine saying no.

I realized I fell in love with them when I didn't mind the three o'clock screaming. Giani had this pterodactyl scream. So it was like being stuck on Jurassic Park at three o'clock in the morning. You'd just look at that little face and she was trying so hard to breathe, so hard to be heard that you just can't not help saying, 'here you are; you're okay.' I didn't mind Cody puking. I didn't mind the challenges. First, it was an adjustment. I realized this feeling I had when I was advocating for them, and forcing my way, and getting what I needed, it wasn't 'it's my responsibility, I signed a contract.' It was I loved them. And I would fight the line for them. Your mother always says, you know when you love somebody you'll realize it. It was that feeling of... oh so this is what that is... There is no mountain too high, no river too deep. I will do it. I will do anything for them. I love them and that's what it means to be a mother.

I am a single parent. I'm fortunate to get support from my family, my siblings. My brother and I live in the same building. So he's on the first floor and often they run away to his house. So I get support from him then there's my niece Robin who's 20 and she gives me a lot of support. She did some training to help with special needs children. So I get support from them and my sister she has a special needs daughter, Susan, so I get support from them too, I'm very fortunate to have family that supports me.

Little City as helped support and provided me with whatever I needed. If I said well she needs to see a specialist, they would help me get that. If I couldn't get in on my own they would call and push it through and I'm be able to get in to see a specialist. I had the foundation of Little Cities saying, "If you can't do it call us and we'll do it for you; we will help you to do this or guide you to do that." So the support of Little City of getting through just cutting through bureaucracy is just a huge help. Their ability to gently but firmly push through has gotten me into see specialist for both of them that I would have had to wait months for.

They both have special needs so they see doctors more and more often, more and more specialists. As I said, Cody had digestive problems. Giania has tumors so she has some tumor tactile functions, some drug exposure, some alcohol exposure. They both have special issues outside the "normal child." So, but Little Cities provided me with the waivers and with assistance so when I need that specialist or need that special formula or need this they provided me with that.

Well to take care of myself while I'm doing this I write. And so my schedule is once they are in bed, they are in bed usually by 8:30 - 9:00, at some point they both just drop. Usually twelve to two I write. And this gives me an outlet, that relaxes me. I'm in bed by 2:30, you're up by 7:30 and you do it all over again. But writing is a tremendous outlet. Then I have as I said, support if like if I want to just get away for an hour, I'll go to the movies. My niece will provide respite care for them. I like just to wander and window shop so just something that will take me away and just give that break and that fresh air you need because you do need it no matter how much you love someone. You do need that step away so that you don't become run down and you don't become worn down. And you take that breath and you come back and you find that even if she's screaming and he's saying I don't want you to go anywhere. You can handle it because you had that time away. So that has helped a lot.

The biggest challenge in trying to meet their needs has been trying to understand them. Before, I'd only read about fetal alcohol exposure of fetal alcohol poisoning or birth defects. I read about it. You volunteer at Easter Seals, you send the check once a year, but actually being exposed to it and seeing children with those needs. That has been a challenge. Living in the moment of them. It's abstract. You read about it. You hear about it. You donate time for it. You donate money for it. But actually living it. Living the tremors. Living the after effects of it. Living the addiction of it. Getting accustomed to it. And working them through it. Actually being exposed to it has been the biggest challenge and knowing how to help them through it.

If Giani didn't have my home I would like to think someone else would have stepped forward and took the care that I have taken. I would like to think that someone else would have been as loving and supportive of her. I don't want to think long term where her needs are not met; where she isn't getting the help that she needs; where she isn't being helped to grow; to develop getting the therapy she needs to be the person she's going to be.

Think about it. It is not something to undergo lightly. It is not something you can do for six months and toss off. It is a lifetime commitment. Because children with special needs even though they might go out, they may have their own families, or their own lives, they will always be attached to you. And there will always be that invisible string. So advise any family to think about it. To really seriously think about it. It is not like having a typical child. It is not something that at the age of 18 right off to the next one. Make sure you understand the ramifications; it's going to have on the entire family on your life because this is not a 9-5, this is 24/7. And to think about, is this something that I really want to do. I think that once you do it you will be rewarded in ways I can't describe. But it is not an easy task. But I don't think it is an impossible one.

They are both incredibly funny. They're smart. Given the least bit of encouragement. They will try anything. They fall down, they both have some issues standing and walking. They fall down they get up again. I look at them and as they grow I think this is going to be one hell of a person. She can be that doctor; he can be this politician; he can be that lawyer. The reward is knowing that you're going to get every opportunity to do what you want to do. And if you want to work as a sanitation worker that's fine if that's what you want. But you're going to get the opportunity to go to Harvard if you want. You're going to get it. It's going to be your choice. And the reward is going to be knowing that I did everything I could possibly do to help you find who you are and what you're going to be. I will never ever have to look back and say I wish, I should've I could've. Because I don't wish that I'd done anything differently. The reward is seeing them be and knowing they're going to be the people they were meant to be.

Chapter Twenty One

NOLA SAYNE
KENNESAW, GA

And then there were times, I just didn't wanna go. This is a long, boring drive and it's a long, boring emotional drive sometimes and there are days I just didn't wanna face it. I just didn't wanna go see my son laying in that bed, try to be happy, try to be cheerful and I didn't feel happy and cheerful.

I've been driving to Montgomery for 13 years. By myself, with my husband, with my kids, my other kids, with friends… I've done it during the week, weekdays, at night, in the rain. One of the reasons that I picked Montgomery was because I figured the weather would never be bad and I would always be able to get to Zach if I needed to cause it doesn't really snow down here. Been making the trip a long time, watch things grow, roads widened and the city is growing. Outside of Montgomery we watched the greyhound track go up, we've eaten at a lot of restaurants all the way down through Georgia and Alabama… I have to say when we finally get Zach back to Georgia; I don't think I'll ever really wanna come back to Montgomery again. It's nothing against Montgomery, but I just don't think I'll ever come back here again. It's a long trip and a lot of driving.

I guess it's been about a year since Georgia Advocacy Office contacted me. They found me, and they explained to me that there are a couple of waiver programs that Zach would qualify for, so that process is rolling right now. I've submitted almost all of the paperwork I needed to the state of Georgia, however, the state of Georgia told me that I need to or Zach needs to be a resident of Georgia in order for him to qualify for any of the waivers so we're kinda at a standstill right now. The Georgia Advocacy Office has been working with the Georgia Council on

Developmental Disabilities and they're trying to figure out how we can deal with that particular requirement of the residency issue. So I don't know if be bringing Zach to a geriatric facility and getting his residency.

I had to talked to Katie lately about the funding too, funding was supposed to be released in October, so I'm really sure where funding is, so we're just kinda stalled right now. But when we do get into Georgia we're looking at the host home option, where he would actually live in someone's home, with an RN, and that person would care for him 24/7 and be a new part of our family and hopefully we would go get to see Zach as much as we wanted. When there are emergencies we wouldn't have to drive this far to get to him. We would be able to get to him on time. It would make our lives a great deal easier if he were at home and it would certainly make him happier to have everybody visiting, to have more than just me and Jeff visiting all the time.

One of the worse trips I remember, I got a call at midnight or one o'clock in the morning. I had to pack and go. They were doing the construction on I-85 and had it down to one lane. They had the little cement temporary walls up on both sides and it was raining and dark and big ol' semis. I always felt by the grace of God I made it all the way without having any sleep and driving at night in the rain, in that situation. Cause I don't even remember going from point A to point B. Those trips are emotional and I'm trying to get there as fast as I can without killing somebody or getting killed, getting a ticket. Those trips were always very difficult. And, I guess he's been in the hospital fifteen times, maybe, fifteen or twenty times since he's been there. One time we drove up, pulled up into the parking lot at Father Walters, there's an ambulance parked outside and I said, oh no, I hope they're gonna be ok. I wonder what child that is and they brought Zach out on a gurney as we were walking past the ambulance. And, we just went straight to the hospital. I felt incredibly guilty about putting my ten-year old son in a facility 180 miles away from me.

There were nights when I would drive down like Friday after work. There was one time in particular, it was after Jeff and I were dating, and I was driving down, it was Friday after work, it was raining, and I was really tired. I was crying. I remember talking to Jeff on the phone on the way down and I was gonna check into the hotel, try to relax for a little bit when I got there. I was just really down. It can be a very depressing trip, and, depending on how he is when I get there, if he's not feeling well or if he's not responsive, if he's really tired and just sleeping a lot and I feel like he might not even realize that I had come to see him. That makes me sad and then sometimes when he doesn't seem to, feel very good, I hate leaving him, it's hard to leave him. I don't know, and then sometimes, I handle it well and I'm fine and it's just routine, but sometimes it just really gets to me. Typically when we take someone down that doesn't go often, like if I take one of our other kids or something and he hears them talking, he'll stay awake and he'll be very alert and reactive to conversation, but because Jeff and I come so frequently, it's not really exciting for him to see us, I guess, or he's just really comfortable and relaxed around us, not sure which one it is. But he usually acknowledges us somehow, that we're there.

The first time that I made the trip to what was then Father Walters, I lived in Lawrenceville, Georgia. I went down to check it out several times before I actually admitted Zach there. The very first time I went down there with my older son, Josh, and a friend of mine. We drove down to look at the facility and spoke with the Director of Nursing there, took a little tour, and found it to be clean, and found the kids to be happy, and healthy and they all looked pretty good. I went down one more time after that at a different time of day, a different day during the week. I tried to get there really, really early to see during the shift change and how they were gonna be with the kids. It was busy and bustling and everybody looked the same as they looked last time; everybody looked clean, everybody looked happy and healthy.

The day that I took him to Father Walters was just a very difficult day. I took the day off of work. I let my older son, Josh, stay out of school. My best friend, Rebel, went with me. We drove Zach down to Father Walters and my ex-husband happened to be there, he was in the parking lot with his dad, waiting for me, and he was trying to make some trouble to say that I didn't have the right to put Zach there, but I had full legal and physical custody. And I actually brought my divorce papers in anticipation of him showing up. So when I got there, the Director of Nursing, he had already spoken to the Director of Nursing, she had asked me, did I have custody and all, and I did, and I showed her the divorce papers, and, so we brought Zachary in and they had his bed and they told me where his room was. It was close to the front of the facility. It was a couple of rooms down on the right. So we went and put him in his bed and got him all cozy. Rebel took my car keys and handed them to my ex-husband and said, "Why don't you unload the car?" Which was great. So, we just sat with him for a while and I cried a lot. I don't think I stopped crying the whole time, the Director of Nursing took me into her office and she had me sign papers and went over their regulations and we went over patient's rights that sort of thing. We finally left later that evening, and, I just remember just crying the whole time.

I took the next day off of work, I was very, very depressed and I stayed home and let my son stay home with me and we just kinda hung out together. We did go to the grocery store that day and it was the first time going to the grocery store without Zach and typically a trip with Zach was loading up his diaper bag, making sure I had supplies, diapers and food and wipes and all the typical stuff you take for a baby, even though he was ten years old at the time I put him in Father Walters. I had all this extra stuff, medicine, whatever... I was always prepared just in case there was an emergency. If we broke down or if something happened, I wanted to make sure that I had plenty of stuff on hand for Zach if I needed it. So, we didn't have to do all that. Josh and I, that first day, we were on our own and it was kinda strange. We just got in the car and went to the grocery store like other people did, and I just can't explain how odd that was. Then we came home and we just, I think we just sat around and watched TV and watched movies all day and, cried a lot and, just kinda hung out together and, that was the beginning.

When we took Zach to Father Walters he only weighed thirty pounds at ten years old; which is kinda what lead to all of this. He had pneumonia seven times in one year and we took him to a gastroenterologist and found out that he was aspirating his food. Also found out that he had very severe reflux which lead to a surgery, so he had to have a feeding tube put in and he also had a procedure called a Nissen Fundoplication which is where they wrap the top of the stomach around the bottom of the esophagus to keep the reflux from coming up into his esophagus. And after the surgery, he started to gain about a pound a week. He was on a liquid diet now through his tube feedings and he was gaining weight rapidly so he was getting a little harder to handle. At thirty pounds and ten years old he moved a lot, although he was somewhat atrophied. For example, I put him on a pallet on the floor, which was kinda the easiest place to put him, because he can't sit up. So I didn't really have a chair or seat that I could put him in. Even when I fed him, I put him in my lap and face him away from me and I would feed him backwards. I couldn't put him in a highchair because he'd fall over. And when I would give him a bath, I would sit in the bathtub with him and just sit him in my lap and bathe him that way. So, when I'd put him on the floor, I'd put some blankets and some toys around him and lay him on the floor and you could get him laughing if you whispered in his ear, or you tickled him or whatever and he would laugh and he would kick his feet. And he did this little scissor kick with his feet, and he'd get to laughing so hard he'd lose his breath and then he'd pick back up and laugh some more and, so he would do things like that. And when he was fussy, he went through a little Terrible Two's kinda stage a little later. Maybe about three or four, if I'd lay him down, for example, on his little pallet and I'd go into the kitchen to cook, he'd be upset cause I wasn't in the room with him so he'd make a lot of noises, shouts and grunts, and I'd tell him that he'd have to be patient. I'd tell him to stop doing that. My pediatrician said it's one thing to have a child with a disability child, it's another thing to have an obnoxious child with a disability. So she said I needed to treat him just like I treated my other child and he needed scolding sometimes just like the other one. So, he laughed, cried when he was upset, but when we took him to Father Walters things did change a lot. For one thing, I was very depressed and he was very depressed because of all the contact. He sat in my lap when he ate, he sat on my lap when he took a bath and he slept with me quite often because he was sick and I wanted to keep an eye on him. So we were always attached, and then all of a sudden he's completely gone, and I'm completely gone from him, and so he's now at Father Walters in his little bed. And then he did go to school and all but they told me after the first year, they didn't tell me this at the time, but after the first year they said that he had been quite depressed, and, not sure why they didn't tell me at the time. I think because they knew that I was depressed too. At first, it really was emotional. It was just really hard. He's twenty-three now, he's a man.

Our other kids were young and we would take them with us, and, they didn't really like going, no kid likes to go to a nursing home or a hospital. Sometimes they would put up a bit of a fight about that, not much. But it was very emotional and I felt an obligation at the time to go every other weekend, at least. And I remember the very first time something came up and it didn't fit with our schedule or something and I was going to miss going that day, and I just remember having a miserable rotten day because I didn't go see Zach and I felt horribly guilty and, felt it was so wrong that I didn't make it that time. And then there were times, I just didn't wanna go. This is a long, boring drive and it's a long, boring emotional drive sometimes and there are days I just didn't wanna face it. I just didn't wanna go see my son laying in that bed, try to be happy, try to be cheerful and I didn't feel happy and cheerful, and there's still days when I just don't wanna go but it's not as painful as it was the first time.

And traveling with him was dangerous cause we would lay him across the backseat and strap him with as many seatbelts as we could strap him in with and wrap him in blankets so that the seatbelts weren't binding on him because he can't sit up. There's no car seat big enough for him. He's about a hundred fifteen pounds at this point and he got up to a hundred pounds within a couple years after he was there. So it was just dangerous and difficult to transport him. I remember the last time I brought him home, I had him strapped in the backseat and I was riding in the HOV lane hoping that I wasn't gonna get pulled over but thinking, "Well I got more than one person in here," It did get difficult to bring him home.

131

The holidays were very difficult. When he was younger we certainly wanted to include him in all the holidays. We have Jeff's family to consider and then we have my family to consider, so then we did bring him home and it was trying to cart him back and forth while he was home to other people's houses. Yeah, and when he finally got there he was just really fragile. He had had several broken bones one year; his femur broke several times just when he was getting dressed, and, that's when I gotta little bit scared about moving him, I got a little bit concerned about should we even try to put him in the car and keep doing this trip with him.

Things would come up and it's hard every other Saturday to set that day aside. I mean you miss out doing chores and running errands and doing things like that so, you know, Jeff would stay home to take care of things and sometimes went by myself and sometimes friends would go with me. I guess four or five years ago, we started moving to every third weekend instead of every other weekend. I remember when I first leased my Toyota Rav that I had, right before Zach went to live at Father Walters. I was only allowed so many miles a year. When Zach ended up at Father Walters it's 180 miles one way. So, I started putting all these miles on my leased car and when I turned it in I had to pay like twenty-six hundred dollars or something because I had put so many miles on it from going down there. We've probably stopped at every single exit between our house and Zach's exit in Montgomery for gas, bathroom, food, something.

I always take off work on his birthday. I always see him on his birthday. Haven't missed one, and will not miss a birthday. Christmas we used to do. We've done Christmas Day in the past, and typically now, we do Christmas Eve and we take him his presents and spend that day with him, after we quit bringing him home. We went down on Thanksgiving Day and the only thing open was Waffle House, so we had our Thanksgiving at Waffle House on the way home, and it was funny cause we were riding along looking at all the houses with lights on thinking all those people have turkeys and stuffing. Think we can pull up

and knock on the door see if we could get some turkey? That was
funny...

Chapter Twenty Two

ESSIE EVAN
DONALSONVILLE, GA

I become furious. Upset. Angry...not at him, but within myself and the medical professionals that are taking care of him when I make my complaints to them, they hear me but they are not listening.

My name is Essie Evans. My son name Cornelius Evans. I have a special needs child with multiple diagnoses. He is non-verbal, non-ambulatory; diagnosed with Mitochondrial Encephalomyopathy , and also scoliosis of the back.

Cornelius had surgery, August of '09 at Scottish Right Hospital, under Dr. Fabregas care; he's an orthopedic surgeon for Scoliosis. I was told he was putting in a spinal infusion to straighten the curve out in his back.

I thought at one time it was going pretty good; I thought at that time it was doing well, but I was concerned about when Dr. Fabergas released my child from Scottish Right Hospital, he didn't send me home with the adequate VNA nurse to come out to check the wounds, for pressure points in his back, and I was concerned about that.

This was after major surgery. So after two weeks, I started calling Dr. Fabregas out at Meridian Mark in Atlanta, and explained to him that Cornelius seemed to be not doing very well. He's running a fever and just doing very poorly and I asked to bring him by there so he could take a look at him.

I was speaking also to his coordinator and she was supposed to be relaying a message to Dr. Fabregas, and she said she was at that time, and she told me "Dr. Fabregas, does not give medication for a fever, he takes care of the pain". I said, well, right now he's running a fever and something else was going on, so he definitely need to come back out there; let Dr. Fabregas look at him to see what's going on.

134

They never would get me out there. He just kept refusing to say, "let's get'em back out here and let's see what's going on."

So I wound up calling his pediatrician in Dothan and explained my situation to him, and how Cornelius' fever was up so high, and how he was breathing, and skin coming off of his ear and everything like that, puss coming out of his back, so he asked me to bring him in and so we got him over there and he stayed less than 48 hours and did a workup on him and had enough time to do a cultural on him, and told me the next day he needs to be transported by ambulance to Scottish Right, and we left out that Thursday night going back to Scottish Right Hospital.

So he started making phone calls to Dr. Fabregas, letting him know what's going on and he needed to be in Atlanta, and the next day before they got us out there to Atlanta; we got about 9:30 or 10 o'clock that night by ambulance, code 3, and as soon as we got him out there, the doctor had been talking back and forth with Dr. Fabregas, and when Dr. Fabregas came in and looked at him; just listened to his breathing before he even checked his back, he said, "My goodness, how long has he been like this?", and I said, "for the last two weeks. I've been calling you trying to inform you about what's going on; speaking with your coordinator, leaving you voice messages about Cornelius and he wasn't doing very well."

So he looked at him that night and first thing he told me..."Mrs. Evans, I really got to get him into surgery right away tonight, and the thing is, that I cut his whole back open before, I don't know how bad the infection is, so what we're going to do, we're going to go in and start cutting and we'll let you know how bad it is, but most likely, with them looking like this, we're going to have to cut his back all the way back open.

I was like, "You're kidding me?"

So we really didn't have time to discuss everything. We had to get him into surgery that night and he went into surgery that night and came out on intensive care pediatric on a breathing machine, and different medication they was giving him, etcetera. He didn't wake up for like nine days. His blood pressure dropped severely; they had him on several

135

blood pressure medications, but Dr. Fabregas continued to take care of him.

They finally sent in an infection doctor to start running samples on what's going on and what type of antibiotics would best fit him.

During that time when he did the first surgery on Cornelius back in August of '09, when he came out of OR he came out with fever, and that raised a red flag right then and there that something gotta be wrong, we just gave this child 3 liters of someone else blood, plus we went to the bone bank and put human bones in his back -- they didn't give me that knowledge they just said, that they lost him in OR because he lost all of his blood back in OR.

I didn't get that part of the information until later, so they should have took a culture from the human bone they put in his back - back in August '09, by now they could have ruled out Mercer in that bone, and they didn't and they would have ruled that out then we would have known definitely that it was the hardware.

We went out for several visits after he had had the surgery and everything like that, and we were talking, and he said, "Ms. Evans you know he lost three liters of blood; it was a major surgery he had, plus I had to go to the bone bank and put bones in his back?" I said, "What you mean you put bones in his back, you didn't tell me that. I only signed for you to do a spinal infusion and you explained to me when you do that you would chop his bones away and you would replace his bones."

And I said, "If you put human bones in his back, why didn't you notify me and give me an option to say well, "Ms. Evans he's in critical condition. We got the blood back in him, but now my thing is that we either need to use artificial bones or human bones."

I didn't get that option, and the first I would have said: "Well, have you all had time to cross-match; is it a marrow match completely and you know that definitely it's a match?"

I didn't know at that time, but when he came out of surgery, I knew something wasn't right after he had the surgery he had to go back in two weeks after the first surgery back in August, then, when they went back in to flush him out, the bones in his lower back was just coming up, comin', coming up, and I said, "OK, well then, why are they coming up?" He said, "They didn't take."

I said, "They didn't take?"

He said, "The Mercer was eatin' them up."

I said, OK, if the Mercer was eating the bones up, why didn't you all do a biopsy on the bone that you put in his back back in '09, that way we would have had this cleared up.

Now is it a bone infected or is it the hardware infected?

The Mercer is a severe staph infection and it eats the flesh. It eats his flesh to where it take over his white blood cells and begin to take over his blood cells and get up to thirty-five thousand, that's where we caught him at, thirty-five hundred, which it should been down to like 9, 10, 15 on the white blood count.

When you get at thirty-five thousand it's just like it's a bacteria and it just eat up what they had put in. And that's what they found. This was all in '09. Dr. Fabregas asked me, and told me: "His hip is dislocated severely and we need to do surgery on that."

And I said, "How can you do surgery on his hip and we just got his back, and his back not even well yet; he's still on antibiotics for 6-9 months, and until the back is completed then we can't do the hip."

And I said, "As a matter of fact, at the same time, I also went out and got two other opinions on the back to make sure what we need to do for the back before we can move any further."

And I shared that information with Dr. Fabregas about what Dr. Marcus said and Dr. Burkus said from the Hughston Clinic of Columbus, and I took him to Schriners in Tampa where he's been going ever since he was like, 2 years of age. They had a spine doctor out there and his opinion was, "Ms. Evans, we do have to wait a year, because if they put anything else in his body that Mercer just gonna continue eat him up. It's not even gonna make any difference. You give him one year, then you tell this doctor, early on, when he goes back in, he need to take the hardware out. The hardware is contaminated."

So I shared that with Dr. Fabregas, and he told me, "If they want it out, why don't they take it out."

And I said, "That was just their opinion and just like you got yours. I trust these doctors. My son been with them many years now, when they tell me something, I believe what they tell me."

And I said, "They got paper work and they did X-rays and MRIs and everything else on his back, and they even see how you have the rod in his back. They had to order and make a special wheelchair for him to sit in until that rod was completed in his back."

That was the main thing Dr. Burkus was concerned about.

Honestly, I couldn't put my fingers on it at that time, knowing my son's condition, even he had talked to me, if he go back in and do another major surgery on Cornelius and this time it's going to take 8 to 9 months of healing and not 8 to 6 weeks, and I said, "Why would you want to go back in and do a hip surgery so quick and he's not healed from the back?"

So, I told him, I didn't want him to do that, but my thing was that, if he could just put the back surgery on the back burner and do a hip surgery and just take the bone out, and then we have more information to go on, it would just raise up more questions to see if the Mercer going to get in his hip and if it's going to go further.

So he thought if he take care of the hip and leave the back alone, then I'll forget about the back and I'll focus on just the hip, but I told him no, that wasn't a good idea.

We had to take care of the back first. I didn't have any choice. It was a medical necessity. After I got the second opinion from Dr. Burkus at the Hughston Clinic, he explained to me and showed me the X-rays on how Cornelius' spine is going; it goes in the position of your head, and the rod is coming out in the opposite direction. He also explained to me about the hardware in his lower hip need to be cut back. The rod kept coming through and I kept running him back and forth to Dr. Fabregas, and asking him, would he be able to go in and correct that before it break through, and they told me, Dr. Fabregas said; "Well, let's just try to hold out that year and see what happens."

138

I said, "But, at the same time, he's feeling a lot of pain from that rod coming through his back, and you sending visiting nurses out to help me keep check on it and keeping his wound clean and taken care of."

We had to wait that one year. When that one year anniversary came around then he decided that we can go head on and soldered the rod off, and bent it and wrapped it up so it won't be sticking through his back.

August 13th, that's what happened. That was on Friday, the 13th, and we were released Saturday, the 14th without no pain medicine; no antibiotics, no nothing.

Dr. Fabregas didn't prescribe anything. He had the pain doctor to come in, Dr. Mahike, to come in and Dr. Mahike wrote a prescription for Clonidine , and I explained to Dr. Mahike he's already on Clonidine from his neurologist. Dr. Mahike also wrote a prescription called Melatonin , so I came home and find out through my pharmacy, what is this Melatonin. I already know what Clonidine is, for agitation, lowers your blood pressure, or for different things, but it was nothing for pain.

So, the pharmacy told me, "Ms. Evans, Melatonin is just like a Tylenol PM just given to put him to sleep. So I called back and I told Dr. Fabregas, I said, "What do you mean that he given me Clonidine and Melatonin, so he and the doctor had a dispute, or had conversation during that time before we left, and I said, "You need to make it clear to Dr. Mahake, the pain clinic doctor that this child just had back surgery and he should be going home with pain medicine and antibiotics."

And I didn't hear back from Dr. Fabregas. Dr. Mahaki just came in and said, "This is what he wrote up and this is what the nurse brought me." And we were discharged.

This was like the 2nd; the first week after surgery he was in excruciating pain and had drainage coming out of his back and the nurse would come out to change it, but some time before she get here, I would have to change a day, and she would change a day, but if he got too much drainage, I'm not going to let it sit on his back. They asked me not to let it sit there but just hold it in a bag until the nurse get there, but go on and change that bandage on his back.

So I said, "I need for you to make sure you're writing all of this down and reporting it back to Dr. Fabregas," and I said, "Make sure you understand at the same time, they are not giving him anything for pain; document that." So she started calling Dr. Fabregas. I started calling Dr. Fabregas, and calling the pain center and etcetera. They just refused to give him pain meds and antibiotics. They started out from prior surgery when the rod started coming through early '09 on Percocet and to help his hip, but I had told them the Percocets are not enough. He's in excruciating pain.

I met back with Dr. Fabregas and he said, "I'm going to get you to the pain clinic, 'cause I don't write narcotics."

And I said, "But you the surgeon you have every right to write a prescription that your patient needs, and then there's going to have to come a day on appointment time when we need to get to that pain clinic, so what are you going to do then?"

And that was one of the times when you came out with your camera crew and he had said he was not going to write me any more pain medicine, and he said, "No I didn't tell you that; what do you need?"

I said, "I've been calling you for about a week or so, and you told your coordinator that you not going to give me anything." "Oh, no, no, I didn't say that! Tell me what do you need?"

That's when you were out there with your cameras and he started writing him Percocet for him to take. They changed the medication to Oxycodone, while he was in the hospital. The nurses were writing up their reports. The doctors were looking at it every day.

The pain doctor never did show up. The neurologist never did show up. The pediatrician doctor never did show up. Only Dr. Davido, Dr. Exelrod showed up, Dr. Harris, which was the infection doctor showed up.

For 15 years, I've been watching Cornelius for 15 years. We have learned to communicate through gestures, through his hands, and his sounds and his actions. If he's not smiling or he's whining and patting his hands too much, and pulling at his ear or pulling at his stomach, to try to let me know "momma something is wrong; talk to me; do something about it."

I just keep watching him and watching, and I say, if I get three of the same sounds in a row, I know something is wrong. If I get four sounds in the same row, I know it's time to get up and go check to make sure that whatever it is, what's wrong with Cornelius.

He'll let you know that he's in pain from day to day, because I do this 24/7.

He squeals and whines out and he'll start...he'll get very agitated, and start trembling sometime he'll start having seizures behind it, or sometimes he'll just let you know that I'm not comfortable, and just "UH! UH! UH!" squeal.

And he'll have a frown on his face, in the doctor's office they have like, on a chart you can look at the pain level if a child smiling a certain degree and goes up, goes down. If my child is not smiling and responding when I talk to him, he'll goo-goo and ghi-ghi back talking to me, but when he stop goo-goo and ghi, talking to me at all, I know something is wrong.

I become furious. Upset. Angry...not at him, but within myself and the medical professionals that are taking care of him when I make my complaints to them, they hear me but they are not listening.

It's a difference between hearing something or hearing someone and listening; when you're listening you begin to respond to do something about it.

So, I'm highly upset. I'm past upset. I have to have counseling as often as I can possibly get into my psychologist to keep my sanity going, on nerve pills and just trying to hold on to what I felt like I have left in me for Cornelius and myself and for other families that are without a voice, I could be that voice for them.

They gave me a bottle of sixty Oxycodone 5mg. He left the hospital taking one every three hours. There's a 24 hour period in a days time which mean he take eight tablets. On the seventh day, he's got...that's fifty-six...four more and that's not enough to go into the next day; that's not going to complete the next day, and I was asked to call the pain clinic

141

within a week's time or before I run out and the thing is now, they were sending him Percocet, faxing the Percocet over, but they wrote a prescription for the Oxycodone.

Cornelius started getting sick, and the doctor's wouldn't listen to me, so I had to have the ambulance come rush Cornelius to a local hospital, and Dr. Fabregas told them to do all the blood work and everything they need to do, and to give him a call back and he'll take it from there.

The doctor at the local hospital did everything Dr. Fabregas asked him to do; called him back and said, "This child needs to be in Atlanta."

Ain't nothing else I can do. The test is right here. Every culture we read out is negative. Only thing else coming up, I had a culture dye done on his back, it will take forty-eight hours to have that back but everything else is ruled out so this has got to be coming from his back. I'm looking at the puss and the infection and the pain this child is in, so Dr. Fabregas said he was going to accept Cornelius to Scottish Right, but he never did.

I called this doctor in Donalsonville, Dr. Harley, who is the on-call doctor that took over Cornelius care during that time and while Cornelius was up there, he kept communicating with Dr. Fabregas and he said, "Ms. Evans, Dr. Fabregas won't take Cornelius through the ER; he wants you to bring Cornelius by ambulance to his office."

Paramedics came to the hospital, they realized where he was going, they said, "We cannot transport a critical patient to a facility like a business like Dr. Fabregas' office, but we can transport him to the ER."

So Dr. Harley kept trying to get Dr. Fabregas to accept Cornelius in the ER, but he kept refusing to accept him in the ER. Finally, they kept telling me; Dr. Harley and the nurse kept telling me "Ms. Evans we not going home tonight until we get some results; somebody is going to have to take this child in because we have done everything we know to do, and that's it."

Finally, I was told that a doctor had accepted him in. I didn't know the exact name of who accepted him in, but when we got out there to Atlanta that night, Dr. Axelrod, who works side-by-side with Dr. Fabregas. Dr. Axelrod came in and looked at him, and said, "Ms. Evans we need to get him in to surgery right away."

I said, "What you mean in surgery right away?" I said, "Where is Dr. Fabregas?" "Well, he, he off right now."

And I told him, just like this, God, I was upset. I had one nerve left after waiting, and I said, "I be damn if he home in the bed. If he is you go call him and you tell him to get his ass out of the bed and get to the hospital, Now! I want to see him face to face, man to man because he allowed my son to stay in Donaldsonville for almost 48 hours before I got a doctor to accept him in and these doctors, all of them work in the same building."

And Dr. Axelrod ran out and finally got Dr. Fabregas in. And I told Dr. Fabregas, I said, "Where do you come off?"

This was maybe about 10 or 12 that night, I think it was. At least about 12 when he was admitted under Dr. Denis Davido care at the hospital.

I told him and Dr. Axelrod, I said, "Dr. Fabregas, you started this. You have been with my son over three to four years now, so you know him very well. What makes you think you can send a child home with the type of surgery you had given him and refuse to send antibiotics and refuse to send pain medicine, and I'm like how dare you."

I really don't want to talk to you tonight. I don't want to have anything else to do with you tonight.

And the social worker came to me and said, "Ms. Evans, he need to go into surgery."

Then Dr. Axelrod came in and said, "Ms. Evans, he do need surgery."

I said; "I can understand that and I respect that and I'm not denying that he don't need it, but before he go into surgery, I asked him what time would surgery be scheduled, because I would like to call a conference with all the personnel that I had been speaking to." He said, "Maybe between 11 or 12, 1 o'clock, I really don't know right off."

So I went on and the social worker got all the personnel involved and we had that conference. I asked Dr. Fabregas to be there but he chose not to be there. I have a list of everybody's name that was there at the meeting.

I explained to them what happened, what had went on and I wanted to know why and how could you all allow this doctor to do what he did and then not be accounted for it?

So I wanted answers. I can't call the social worker and get him to do anything. Patient representative I have called and spoke with them they not doing anything. I spoke with the pain coordinator and he going to pretend as if he was a nurse or doctor and going to tell me how to administer medication.

So they took bone out of his back on, I think it was on the 29th. First they got the blood culture two days later, stating that he has MRSA. After they went in to flush, I asked the infection doctor; I asked Dr. Davido to make sure the bone that Dr. Fabregas put in that part of that bone come out to send to genetics lab to find out what's going on.

So when the test came back and Dr. Davido came back in "Oh, Ms. Evans the test is negative."

I said, "Well, I don't know which test that shows, but I got paperwork that proves...don't ask me how I got it...that was just part of a test and that test that came back negative, that's not even what they were looking for. This test going to take 6-8 weeks if not longer. And once this comes back and rule out that Mercer is not in that bone, then it's in the hardware."

So he did admit, "Ms. Evans you could be right, Dr. Fabregas was downstairs that night. You're probably right, the hardware is contaminated."

That's what he told me.

---

[1] Mitochondrial myopathies are a group of neuromuscular diseases caused by damage to the mitochondria-small, energy-producing structures that serve as the cells' "power plants." Nerve cells in the brain and muscles require a great deal of energy, and thus appear to be particularly damaged when mitochondrial dysfunction occurs. Some of the more common mitochondrial myopathies include Kearns-Sayre syndrome, myoclonus epilepsy with ragged-red fibers, and mitochondrial encephalomyopathy with lactic acidosis and stroke-like episodes. The symptoms of mitochondrial myopathies include: muscle weakness or exercise intolerance.